The Incredibly Interesting Psychology Book

DAVID WEBB

www.all-about-psychology.com

ISBN-10: 1484953991

ISBN-13: 978-1484953990

To Louise, Luca and Paolo, with much love

CONTENTS

ABOUT THE AUTHOR

David Webb has a first class honors degree in Psychology and a Masters in Occupational Psychology. For a number of years, he was a lecturer in Psychology at the University of Huddersfield (UK).

He is the writer and host of four websites built around his teaching and research interests. Together these websites receive over 120,000 unique visitors each month and generate over 4 million yearly page views.

An active promoter of psychology through social media his psychology facebook page (facebook.com/psychologyonline) has over 80,000 followers and he is listed by The British Psychological Society among the top psychologists who tweet. His Psychology Student Guide (amazon.com/dp/B009ZC2UOS) published on the Kindle in 2012 is an international #1 Best Seller.

1. INTRODUCTION

"I have no special talents. I am only passionately curious."

(Albert Einstein)

It's nice to have something in common with Albert Einstein! I've had a passionately curious interest in psychology for over 20 years. I began studying psychology in 1990, and I've been teaching psychology in some capacity or another since 1998.

I have also been sharing my passionately curious interest online for a good few years now. Back in the early days I would regularly post on Myspace - I often wonder what happened to Tom!

Then before you could say, Zuckerberg, Charlie bit my finger and what the Hell is a hashtag? Along came Facebook, YouTube and Twitter. These social media giants offer unprecedented opportunities to connect with millions of people around the world, as do the latest platforms on the block, Google+ and Pinterest.

I use one or more of these social networks daily to share my enthusiasm for psychology, and have been doing so for over six years now. That makes quite a back catalog of posts on a wide range of psychological topics. And it is this point that brings me to the thinking behind the book. You see, during this time certain posts have stood out in terms of the response they elicited, be that in number of likes, comments made, how often the post was shared etc - and it is these posts which form the basis for the majority of the material covered in this book.

So What is it About These Posts Then?

They make you think, they have real world relevance, they challenge assumptions, they make you exclaim "Well I never!" Basically, they cover topics that people just find incredibly interesting.

I should add that posts which cover quirky, fun and irreverent topics are also very popular and will also feature in this book, not least because psychology can be a serious business and it's good to remind yourself that there is funny ha ha, as well as funny peculiar.

Who is This Book For?

This book is for anybody interested in psychology whatever their connection with the topic.

If you are a psychology student I hope that this book shows what a great decision you made to study this fascinating subject.

If you are thinking about studying psychology I hope that this book will convince you that you absolutely should.

If you teach psychology I hope that this book will provide you with some engaging content to present in class.

And if you just have a general interest I hope that this book will make you realize that psychology covers a variety of topics which are not only incredibly interesting but also applicable to many people's lives, including your own.

Getting The Most Out of This Book

This book has no set order. Just find a chapter which tickles your fancy and off you go.

Throughout the book you will find links to additional information and resources. You will also come across a chapter or two where I recommend checking out a link before reading on. Obviously this will require you to access the Internet, which you may, or may not be able to do as you are reading this book. With this in mind I have, therefore, included full link URL addresses for your future reference.

Even More Incredibly Interesting Psychology

I intend to add additional sections to the book from time-to-time. If you would like to know about this extra material as soon as it becomes available you can do so by joining the official update list. See following link for details.

www.all-about-psychology.com/interesting-psychology.html

Thank you very much for taking a look at the incredibly interesting psychology book, it's very much appreciated. According to the legendary William James (more on him later) "*The first fact for us then, as psychologists, is that thinking of some sort goes on.*"

Let The Thinking Begin!

2. I CAN READ YOU LIKE A BOOK

Although we have never met before I'm confident that I can accurately tap into and describe aspects of your personality. The reason I'm confident that I can do this is because you can actually tell a great deal about somebody by the books they choose to read. So the fact you have made a conscious decision to get hold of a psychology book tells me in all probability that:

You pride yourself as an independent thinker and do not accept others' statements without satisfactory proof.

You have a great deal of unused capacity which you have not turned to your advantage.

You prefer a certain amount of change and variety and become dissatisfied when hemmed in by restrictions and limitations.

You have a great need for other people to like and admire you.

You have a tendency to be critical of yourself.

While you have some personality weaknesses, you are generally able to compensate for them.

Disciplined and self-controlled outside, you tend to be worrisome and insecure inside.

At times you have serious doubts as to whether you have made the right decision or done the right thing.

You have found it unwise to be too frank in revealing yourself to others.

At times you are extroverted, affable, sociable, while at other times you are introverted, wary, reserved.

Some of your aspirations tend to be pretty unrealistic.

Security is one of your major goals in life.

So How Did I Do?

On a scale of zero (poor) to five (perfect) how would you rate the extent to which my description reveals basic characteristics of your personality?

In most cases this personality sketch consistently receives ratings of 4 or 5 which is very impressive.

Well it would be impressive, except for the fact that my analysis has absolutely nothing to do with what you read. It's simply a demonstration of how people can be misled by a general personality description.

The human susceptibility to interpret broadly applicable statements as uniquely meaningful is often referred to as the *Barnum Effect* named after the celebrated American showman P.T Barnum's famous remark that "*we've got something for everyone*". It is also known as the *Forer Effect* in recognition of Bertram R. Forer's classic research paper into the subject which was published in 1949 under the title "*The Fallacy of Personal Validation: A Classroom Demonstration of Gullibility*."

My favorite aspect to this study is that if Forer had not been out clubbing (albeit clubbing 1940's style!) he may never have conducted his landmark research. I'll let Forer himself explain.

"*Recently the writer was accosted by a night-club graphologist who wished to "read" his handwriting...An amiable discussion ensued, during which the graphologist ventured proof of the scientific basis of his work in that his clients affirmed the correctness of his interpretations. The writer suggested that a psychologist could make a blindfold reading and attain the same degree of verification.* "

Forer was essentially telling the graphologist that his "*clients*" were confirming his interpretations, not because handwriting analysis is able to determine the personality of an individual (it cannot) but rather because the "analysis" simply consists of universally valid personality descriptions. These types of personality descriptions are not only often considered accurate but they are also mistakenly considered unique. As Forer notes:

"*A naive person who receives superficial diagnostic information, especially when the social situation is prestige-laden, tends to accept such information. He is impressed by the obvious truths and may be oblivious to the discrepancies. But he does more than this. He also validates the instrument and the diagnostician.* "

To support this claim Forer conducted a brilliant experiment, the details of which are recorded below.

The following experiment was performed in the writer's class in Introductory Psychology, to demonstrate the ease with which clients may be misled by a general personality description into unwarranted approval of a diagnostic tool. The writer had discussed his Diagnostic Interest Blank (hereafter referred to as DIB) in connection with the role of personal motivational factors in perceptual selectivity.

The DIB consists of a list of hobbies, reading materials, personal characteristics, job duties, and secret hopes and ambitions of one's ideal person. The test is interpreted qualitatively and personality dynamics are inferred along lines similar to projective tests. Class members requested that they be given the test and a personality evaluation. The writer acquiesced.

At the next meeting the 39 students were given DIB's to fill out, and were told that they would be given a brief personality vignette as soon as the writer had time to examine their test papers. One week later each student was given a typed personality sketch with his name written on it. The writer encouraged the expressed desire of the class for secrecy regarding the content of the sketches. Fortunately, this was the day on which a quiz was scheduled; hence it was possible to ensure their sitting two seats apart without arousing suspicion. From the experimenter's point of view it was essential that no student see the sketch received by any other student because all sketches were identical.

The students were unsuspecting. The personality sketch consists of 13 statements. These statements came largely from a news stand astrology book.

The sketch consists of the following items.

1. *You have a great need for other people to like and admire you.*

2. *You have a tendency to be critical of yourself.*

3. *You have a great deal of unused capacity which you have not turned to your advantage.*

4. *While you have some personality weaknesses, you are generally able to compensate for them.*

5. *Your sexual adjustment has presented problems for you.*

6. *Disciplined and self-controlled outside, you tend to be worrisome and insecure inside.*

7. *At times you have serious doubts as to whether you have made the right decision or done the right thing.*

8. *You prefer a certain amount of change and variety and become dissatisfied when hemmed in by restrictions and limitations.*

9. *You pride yourself as an independent thinker and do not accept others' statements without satisfactory proof.*

10. *You have found it unwise to be too frank in revealing yourself to others.*

11. *At times you are extroverted, affable, sociable, while at other times you are introverted, wary, reserved.*

12. Some of your aspirations tend to be pretty unrealistic.

13. Security is one of your major goals in life.

Before the sketches were passed to the students, instructions were given first to read the sketches and then to turn the papers over and make the following ratings:

A. Rate on a scale of zero (poor) to five (perfect) how effective the DIB is in revealing personality.

B. Rate on a scale of zero to five the degree to which the personality description reveals basic characteristics of your personality.

C. Then turn the paper again and check each statement as true or false about yourself or use a question mark if you cannot tell.

Findings

The data show clearly that the group had been gulled. Ratings of adequacy of the DIB included only one rating below 4. Thus the instrument received a high degree of personal validation.

In the evaluation of the sketch as a whole there were five ratings below 4. While a few students were more critical of the sketch than of the DIB, most of them were ready to admit that basic personality traits had been revealed. The number of specific items accepted as true varied among the group from 8 to 13.

All of the students accepted the DIB as a good or perfect instrument for personality measurement. Most of them can be accused of a logical error in accepting the test on such scanty evidence.

In answer to their requests students were informed that the writer had another copy of their sketch and would give it to them after the data were collected. After the papers had been returned to the writer students were asked to raise their hands if they felt the test had done a good job. Virtually all hands went up and the students noticed this.

Then the first sketch item was read and students were asked to indicate by hands whether they had found anything similar on their sketches. As all hands rose, the class burst into laughter. *It was pointed out to them that the experiment had been performed as an object lesson to demonstrate the tendency to be overly impressed by vague statements and to endow the diagnostician with an unwarrantedly high degree of insight.* Similarities between the demonstration and the activities of charlatans were pointed out.

We Are Just As Gullible Today

Forer's findings have been supported on numerous occasions since 1949, a recent example of which was provided by psychological illusionist Derren Brown in his TV series Trick of the Mind.

In a perfectly executed demonstration of the Forer effect Derren Brown took a group of volunteers in London, Los Angeles and Barcelona and asked them to draw around their hand on a piece of paper. On this same piece of paper the volunteers were instructed to write down their birth date and time of birth if known. The volunteers were then asked to take a personal object (but nothing immediately recognizable as theirs) and place it an envelope along with their hand drawing and birth information. Having done this, Derren Brown informed the volunteers that he would now be able to provide each of them with a detailed personality profile.

The Results

Upon receiving their personality profiles, to say that the volunteers were impressed is an understatement. Here are just a few of the comments made.

London Volunteers

"It's unbelievable; I can't believe how accurate it is."

"I can't believe he's analyzing me so accurately."

"It does actually feel so personal it's actually quite difficult for me to share."

Los Angeles Volunteers

"I feel it pretty summed up the way I am."

"Its kinda astounding, I've always believed in something like it, this just kinda confirms it but it also shocks me because I didn't think it would work so well."

"It was shockingly accurate."

Barcelona Volunteers

"It goes into very profound things about my personality."

"75% was so accurate and so personal."

"There are things that are nailed perfectly."

Time To Come Clean

Ever the consummate showman, Derren Brown announces that he would like to try something else. He asks the volunteers to fold up their personality profiles and pass them around the group so that nobody knows which profile they have ended up with. The volunteers are then asked to read the profile to see if they can identify which person it belongs to. At first the volunteers think that by chance that they have ended up reading their own profile again, however, soon the realization begins to dawn that they have in fact all been given exactly the same personality profile!

Why Is This Important?

At the very least the Forer effect should make you think more critically about astrology, fortune telling, graphology and psychic powers. Bear in mind what some of volunteers said after all had been revealed by Derren Brown.

"Had not we have got to this second part I would have walked away from here

thinking you had psychic abilities."

"I won't feel shivers and I will not be afraid of card readers because I know it's a lie...and they are tricking me, and it costs a lot, and it's a big industry, isn't it?"

What Are You Waiting Forer? (Sorry, couldn't resist the play on words!)

Following Bertram Forer's original study many of the students involved asked for a copy of the personality sketch in order to try it out on their friends. Want to test the Forer effect out with your friends or family? If so, all you need is:

1. A (fictitious) way to obtain a personality reading.

Forer used a made-up diagnostic questionnaire, Derren Brown used hand drawings and birth date information and I used the type of books people read.

2. A personality profile.

Remember, the profile must be exactly the same for each person you try this with. You could use or adapt the 13 statements employed by Forer (see above) or you could come up with your own personality profile. Forer, for instance, based his personality sketch on the contents of a news stand astrology book.

If you do decide to construct your own one-profile-fits-all personality sketch but aren't sure whether to include a particular statement, just ask yourself - would this statement apply to most people? If the answer is yes then you are good to go e.g.

You have a tendency to worry but not to excess.

You do get depressed at times but on the whole you are generally cheerful and rather optimistic.

3. An accuracy rating:

Make sure you ask people to rate the extent to which they felt you had been able to accurately read their personality e.g. a % score out of 100.

4. An informed explanation:

Finally, do not forget to tell each person you try this with that their personality reading was just a smoke screen and that the real purpose behind the exercise was to demonstrate the Forer effect i.e. that people tend to interpret broadly applicable statements as uniquely meaningful to them.

Additional Information Links

Read Bertram R. Forer's original research paper in full.

www.all-about-psychology.com/support-files/the-fallacy-of-personal-validation-a-classroom-demonstration-of-gullibility.pdf

Find out more about the incomparable Derren Brown.

www.all-about-psychology.com/derren-brown.html.

3. THE END OF THE WORLD, WHY SMOKING IS COOL AND BELIEVING IS SEEING

I must admit I had a lot of fun with the whole Mayan calendar end of the world thing in 2012. However, that being said, I was also aware that for many people the impending doomsday date was a genuine cause of concern. So much so in fact that NASA scientists felt compelled to help dispel all the myths and baseless rumors.

"NASA has received thousands of emails and calls from members of the public who are concerned, especially young people." (NASA Scientist David Morrison)

To be honest I had completely forgotten that the world was coming to an end until I read a newspaper article with the headline *"Mayan apocalypse: Panic spreads as December 21 nears."*

At the time, two thoughts crossed my mind; firstly, I've got the perfect excuse for not spending much on the Wife's Christmas present this year! And secondly, on the morning of the 22nd December, how would all those people who were convinced that the world was definitely going to end the day before, be coping with the fact that the only thing destroyed on the 21st of December was their strongly held belief.

Enter cognitive dissonance - a robust psychological mechanism which helps resolve states of inner tension triggered by logically inconsistent ways of thinking. As far as inconsistent thinking goes; thinking that the world is definitely going to end on a certain day, only for it to not, is about as inconsistent as it gets. The brilliant psychologist Leon Festinger was acutely aware of this back in 1956 when he infiltrated a group who sincerely believed that the world was about to end but that they would be rescued by a flying saucer on the fateful day.

The reason that this particular prophecy failed according to the group leader was because the group had *"spread so much light"* God had spared the planet. The group then began spreading the good news to non-believers. Now that's classic Cognitive Dissonance!

"Suppose an individual believes something with his whole heart; suppose further that he has a commitment to this belief and that he has taken irrevocable actions because of it; finally, suppose that he is presented with evidence, unequivocal and undeniable evidence that his belief is wrong: what will happen? The individual will frequently emerge, not only unshaken, but even more convinced of the truth of his beliefs than ever before." (Leon Festinger 1956)

Cognitive Dissonance is a great example of a psychological theory with real world applicability. Take smoking for instance; people know it's bad for their health and, therefore, come up with a variety of ingenious defenses to minimize the impact of this tension inducing thought.

But looks cool could just as easily be replaced with

...but helps keep my weight down

...but helps reduces my stress

...but grandpa smoked two packs a day and he lived to be 102

To learn more about the real world relevance of cognitive dissonance check out the following link to listen to a very informative podcast in which host Dr Ginger Campbell. talks with Carol Tavris, PhD about her book *Mistakes Were Made (But Not by Me): Why We Justify Foolish Beliefs, Bad Decisions, and Hurtful Acts.*

traffic.libsyn.com/brainsciencepodcast/43-Books-Tavris.mp3

(*Please note that the discussion relating to cognitive dissonance begins about 16 minutes into the podcast.*)

I love the theory of cognitive dissonance because once you understand the basic concept; you begin to notice it being employed by people all around you in a wide variety of contexts. Remember though, it's not just other people! How often do you employ the cognitive dissonance defense?

Believing is Seeing

A concept closely related to cognitive dissonance is confirmation bias and just like cognitive dissonance once you understand the thinking behind it, you will be amazed by just how common it is.

"*Believing is seeing...Once we have a belief we see the information that will confirm that belief, and we stop seeing what we don't want to see...We want to see evidence that confirms our beliefs, and we want to forget anything that is dissonant or discrepant.*" (Dr. Carol Tavris)

I'm sure you can think of lots of examples where people selectively filter information in this way. My own confirmation bias operates on overdrive when I watch my favorite sports teams play and it's for this reason that I have included the following article.

They Saw A Game: A Case Study

This classic psychology study from 1954 by Albert Hastorf and Hadley Cantril shows how an Ivy League football game was perceived differently by opposing fans. It would go to form the basis for additional research into social cognition and cognitive bias.

On a brisk Saturday afternoon, November 23, 1951, the Dartmouth football team played Princeton in Princeton's Palmer Stadium. It was the last game of the season for both teams and of rather special significance because the Princeton team had won all its games so far and one of its players, Kazmaier, was receiving All-American mention and had just appeared as the cover man on Time magazine, and was playing his last game.

A few minutes after the opening kick-off, it became apparent that the game was going to be a rough one. The referees were kept busy blowing their whistles and penalizing both sides. In the second quarter, Princeton's star left the game with a broken nose. In the third quarter, a Dartmouth player was taken off the field with a broken leg. Tempers flared both during and after the game. The official statistics of the game, which Princeton won, showed that Dartmouth was penalized 70 yards, Princeton 25, not counting more than a few plays in which both sides were penalized.

Needless to say, accusations soon began to fly. The game immediately became a matter of concern to players, students, coaches, and the administrative officials of the two institutions, as well as to alumni and the general public who had not seen the game but had become sensitive to the problem of big-time football through the recent exposures of subsidized players, commercialism, etc. Discussion of the game continued for several weeks.

One of the contributing factors to the extended discussion of the game was the extensive space given to it by both campus and metropolitan newspapers. An indication of the fervor with which the discussions were carried on is shown by a few excerpts from the campus dailies.

For example, on November 27 (four days after the game), the Daily Princetonian (Princeton's student newspaper) said:

This observer has never seen quite such a disgusting exhibition of so-called "sport." Both teams were guilty but the blame must be laid primarily on Dartmouth's doorstep. Princeton, obviously the better team, had no reason to rough up Dartmouth. Looking at the situation rationally, we don't see why the Indians should make a deliberate attempt to cripple Dick Kazmaier or any other

Princeton player. The Dartmouth psychology, however, is not rational itself.

The November 30th edition of the Princeton Alumni Weekly said:

But certain memories of what occurred will not be easily erased. Into the record books will go in indelible fashion the fact that the last game of Dick Kazmaier's career was cut short by more than half when he was forced out with a broken nose and a mild concussion, sustained from a tackle that came well after he had thrown a pass.

This second-period development was followed by a third quarter outbreak of roughness that was climaxed when a Dartmouth player deliberately kicked Brad Glass in the ribs while the latter was on his back. Throughout the often unpleasant afternoon, there was undeniable evidence that the losers' tactics were the result of an actual style of play, and reports on other games they have played this season substantiate this.

Dartmouth students were "seeing" an entirely different version of the game through the editorial eyes of the Dartmouth (Dartmouth's undergraduate newspaper). For example, on November 27 the Dartmouth said:

However, the Dartmouth-Princeton game set the stage for the other type of dirty football. A type which may be termed as an unjustifiable accusation.

Dick Kazmaier was injured early in the game. Kazmaier was the star, an All-American. Other stars have been injured before, but Kazmaier had been built to represent a Princeton idol. When an idol is hurt there is only one recourse—the tag of dirty football. So what did the Tiger Coach Charley Caldwell do? He announced to the world that the Big Green had been out to extinguish the Princeton star. His purpose was achieved.

After this incident, Caldwell instilled the old see-what-they-did-go-get-them attitude into his players. His talk got results. Gene Howard and Jim Miller were both injured. Both had dropped back to pass, had passed, and were standing unprotected in the backfield. Result: one bad leg and one leg broken.

The game was rough and did get a bit out of hand in the third quarter. Yet most of the roughing penalties were called against Princeton while Dartmouth received more of the illegal-use-of-the-hands variety.

On November 28 the Dartmouth said:

Dick Kazmaier of Princeton admittedly is an unusually able football player. Many Dartmouth men traveled to Princeton, not expecting to win—only hoping to see an All-American in action. Dick Kazmaier was hurt in the second period, and played only a token part in the remainder of the game. For this, spectators were sorry. But there were no such feelings for Dick Kazmaier's health. Medical authorities have confirmed that as a relatively unprotected passing and running star in a contact sport, he is quite liable to injury. Also, his particular injuries - a broken nose and slight concussion - were no more serious than is experienced almost any day in any football practice, where there is no more serious stake than playing the following Saturday. Up to the Princeton game, Dartmouth players suffered about 10 known nose fractures and face injuries, not to mention several slight concussions.

Did Princeton players feel so badly about losing their star? They shouldn't have. During the past undefeated campaign they stopped several individual stars by a concentrated effort, including such mainstays as Frank Hauff of Navy, Glenn Adams of Pennsylvania and Rocco Calvo of Cornell. In other words, the same brand of football condemned by the Prince - that of stopping the big man - is practiced quite successfully by the Tigers.

Basically, then, there was disagreement as to what had happened during the "game." Hence we took the opportunity presented by the occasion to make a "real life" study of a perceptual problem. (We are not concerned here with the problem of guilt or responsibility for infractions, and nothing here implies any judgment as to who was to blame).

PROCEDURE

Two steps were involved in gathering data. The first consisted of answers to a questionnaire designed to get reactions to the game and to learn something of the climate of opinion in each institution. This questionnaire was administered a week after the game to both Dartmouth and Princeton undergraduates who were taking introductory and intermediate psychology courses.

The second step consisted of showing the same motion picture of the game to a sample of undergraduates in each school and having them check on another questionnaire, as they watched the film, any infraction of the rules they saw and whether these infractions were "mild" or "flagrant." (The film shown was kindly loaned for the purpose of the experiment by the Dartmouth College Athletic Council. It should be pointed out that a movie of a football game follows the ball, is thus selective, and omits a good deal of the total action on the field. Also, of course, in viewing only a film of a game, the possibilities of participation as spectator are greatly limited).

At Dartmouth, members of two fraternities were asked to view the film on December 7; at Princeton, members of two undergraduate clubs saw the film early in January.

The answers to both questionnaires were carefully coded and transferred to punch cards.

RESULTS

Data from the first Questionnaire below shows the questions which received different replies from the two student populations.

Questions asking if the students had friends on the team, if they had ever played football themselves, if they felt they knew the rules of the game well, etc. showed no differences in either school and no relation to answers given to other questions. This is not surprising since the students in both schools come from essentially the same type of educational, economic, and ethnic background. Summarizing the data we find a marked contrast between the two student groups.

Nearly all Princeton students judged the game as "rough and dirty" - not one of them thought it "clean and fair." And almost nine tenths of them thought the other side started the rough play. By and large they felt that the charges they understood were being made were true; most of them felt the charges were made in order to avoid similar situations in the future.

When Princeton students looked at the movie of the game, they saw the Dartmouth team make over twice as many infractions as their own team made. And they saw the Dartmouth team make over twice as many infractions as were seen by Dartmouth students. When Princeton students judged these infractions as "flagrant" or "mild," the ratio was about two "flagrant" to one "mild" on the Dartmouth team, and about one "flagrant" to three "mild" on the Princeton team.

As for the Dartmouth students, while the plurality of answers fell in the "rough and dirty" category, over one-tenth thought the game was "clean and fair" and over a third introduced their own category of "rough and fair" to describe the action. Although a third of the Dartmouth students felt that Dartmouth was to blame for starting the rough play, the majority of Dartmouth students thought both sides were to blame. By and large, Dartmouth men felt that the charges they understood were being made were not true, and most of them thought the reason for the charges was Princeton's concern for its football star.

When Dartmouth students looked at the movie of the game they saw both teams make about the same number of infractions. And they saw their own team make only half the number of infractions the Princeton students saw them make. The ratio of "flagrant" to "mild" infractions was about one to one when Dartmouth students judged the Dartmouth team, and about one "flagrant" to two "mild" when Dartmouth students judged infractions made by the Princeton team.

It should be noted that Dartmouth and Princeton students were thinking of different charges in judging their validity and in assigning reasons as to why the charges were made. It should also be noted that whether or not students were spectators of the game in the stadium made little difference in their responses.

Data From First Questionnaire

Dartmouth Students (N=163), Princeton Students (N=161)

Question 1

Did you happen to see the actual game between Dartmouth and Princeton in Plamer Stadium this year?

Dartmouth Students

Yes 33% No 67%

Princeton Students

Yes 71% No 29%

Question 2

Have you seen a movie of the game or seen it on television?

Dartmouth Students

Yes, movie 33% Yes, television 0% No, neither 67%

Princeton Students

Yes, movie 2% Yes, television 1% No, neither 97%

Question 3 (Asked of those who answered yes to either or both of above questions.)

From your observations of what went on at the game, do you believe the game was clean and fairly played, or that it was unnecessarily rough and dirty?

Dartmouth Students

Clean and fair 6% Rough and dirty 24% Rough and fair 25% No answer 45%

Princeton Students

Clean and fair 0% Rough and dirty 69% Rough and fair 2% No answer 29%

Question 4 (Asked of those who answered "no" on both of the first questions.)

From what you have heard and read about the game, do you feel it was clean and fairly played, or that it was unnecessarily rough and dirty?

Dartmouth Students

Clean and fair 7% Rough and dirty 18% Rough and fair 14% Don't know 6% No answer 55%

Princeton Students

Clean and fair 0% Rough and dirty 24% Rough and fair 1% Don't know 4% No answer 71%

Combined answers to questions 3 and 4

Dartmouth Students

Clean and fair 13% Rough and dirty 42% Rough and fair 39% Don't know 6%

Princeton Students

Clean and fair 0% Rough and dirty 93% Rough and fair 3% Don't know 4%

Question 5

From what you saw in the game or the movies, or from what you have read, which team do you feel started the rough play?

Dartmouth Students

Dartmouth started it 36% Princeton started it 2% Both started it 53% Neither 6% No answer 3%

Princeton Students

Dartmouth started it 86% Princeton started it 0% Both started it 11% Neither 1% No answer 2%

Question 6

What is your understanding of the charges being made? (Replies do not add to 100% since more than one charge could be given).

Dartmouth Students

Dartmouth tried to get Kazmaier 71% Dartmouth intentionally dirty 52% Dartmouth unnecessarily rough 8%

Princeton Students

Dartmouth tried to get Kazmaier 47% Dartmouth intentionally dirty 44% Dartmouth unnecessarily rough 35%

Question 7

Do you feel there is any truth to these charges?

Dartmouth Students

Yes 10% No 57% Partly 29% Don't know 4%

Princeton Students

Yes 55% No 4% Partly 35% Don't know 6%

Question 8

Why do you think the charges were made?

Dartmouth Students

Injury to Princeton star 70% To prevent repetition 2% No answer 28%

Princeton Students

Injury to Princeton star 23% To prevent repetition 46% No answer 31%

INTERPRETATION: THE NATURE OF A SOCIAL EVENT

It seems clear that the "game" actually was many different games and that each version of the events that transpired was just as "real" to a particular person as other versions were to other people. A consideration of the experiential phenomena that constitute a "football game" for the spectator may help us both to account for the results obtained and illustrate something of the nature of any social event.

Like any other complex social occurrence, a "football game" consists of a whole host of happenings. Many different events are occurring simultaneously. Furthermore, each happening is a link in a chain of happenings, so that one follows another in sequence. The "football game," as well as other complex social situations, consists of a whole matrix of events. In the game situation, this matrix of events consists of the actions of all the players, together with the behavior of the referees and linesmen, the action on the sidelines, in the grandstands, over the loud-speaker, etc.

Of crucial importance is the fact that an "occurrence" on the football field or in any other social situation does not become an experiential "event" unless and until some significance is given to it: an "occurrence" becomes an "event" only when the happening has significance. And a happening generally has significance only if it reactivates learned significances already registered in what we have called a person's assumptive form world.

Hence the particular occurrences that different people experienced in the football game were a limited series of events from the total matrix of events potentially available to them. People experienced those occurrences that reactivated significances they brought to the occasion; they failed to experience those occurrences which did not reactivate past significances. We do not need to introduce "attention" as an "intervening third" (to paraphrase James on memory) to account for the selectivity of the experiential process.

In this particular study, one of the most interesting examples of this phenomenon was a telegram sent to an officer of Dartmouth College by a member of a Dartmouth alumni group in the Midwest. He had viewed the film which had been shipped to his alumni group from Princeton after its use with Princeton students, who saw, as we noted, an average of over nine infractions by Dartmouth players during the game. The alumnus, who couldn't see the infractions he had heard publicized, wired:

Preview of Princeton movies indicates considerable cutting of important part please wire explanation and possibly air mail missing part before showing scheduled for January 25 we have splicing equipment.

The "same" sensory impingements emanating from the football field, transmitted through the visual mechanism to the brain, also obviously gave rise to different experiences in different people. The significances assumed by different happenings for different people depend in large part on the purposes people bring to the occasion and the assumptions they have of the purposes and probable behavior of other people involved. This was amusingly pointed out by the New York Herald Tribune's sports columnist, Red Smith, in describing a prize fight between Chico Vejar and Carmine Fiore in his column of December 21, 1951. Among other things, he wrote:

You see, Steve Ellis is the proprietor of Chico Vejar, who is a highly desirable tract of Stamford, Conn., welterweight. Steve is also a radio announcer. Ordinarily there is no conflict between Ellis the Brain and Ellis the Voice because Steve is an uncommonly substantial lump of meat who can support both halves of a split personality and give away weight on each end without missing it.

This time, though, the two Ellises met head-on, with a sickening, rending crash. Steve the Manager sat at ringside in the guise of Steve the Announcer broadcasting a dispassionate, unbiased, objective report of Chico's adventures in the ring.

Clear as mountain water, his words came through, winning big for Chico. Winning? Hell, Steve was slaughtering poor Fiore.

Watching and listening, you could see what a valiant effort the reporter was making to remain cool and detached. At the same time you had an illustration of the old, established truth that when anybody with a preference watches a fight, he sees only what he prefers to see.

That is always so. That is why, after any fight that doesn't end in a clean knockout, there always are at least a few hoots when the decision is announced. A guy from, say, Billy Graham's neighborhood goes to see Billy fight and he watches Graham all the time. He sees all the punches Billy throws, and hardly any of the punches Billy catches. So it was with Steve.

"Fiore feints with a left," he would say, honestly believing that Fiore hadn't caught Chico full on the chops. "Fiore's knees buckle," he said, "and Chico backs away." Steve didn't see the hook that had driven Chico back.

In brief, the data here indicate that there is no such "thing" as a "game" existing "out there" in its own right which people merely "observe." The "game" "exists" for a person and is experienced by him only in so far as certain happenings have significances in terms of his purpose. Out of all the occurrences going on in the environment, a person selects those that have some significance for him from his own egocentric position hi the total matrix.

Obviously in the case of a football game, the value of the experience of watching the game is enhanced if the purpose of "your" team is accomplished, that is, if the happening of the desired consequence is experienced - i.e. if your team wins. But the value attribute of the experience can, of course, be spoiled if the desire to win crowds out behavior we value and have come to call sportsmanlike.

The sharing of significances provides the links except for which a "social" event would not be experienced and would not exist for anyone.

A "football game" would be impossible except for the rules of the game which we bring to the situation and which enable us to share with others the significances of various happenings. These rules make possible a certain repeatability of events such as first downs, touchdowns, etc. If a person is unfamiliar with the rules of the game, the behavior he sees lacks repeatability and consistent significance and hence "doesn't make sense."

And only because there is the possibility of repetition is there the possibility that a happening has a significance. For example, the balls used in games are designed to give a high degree of repeatability. While a football is about the only ball used in games which is not a sphere, the shape of the modern football has apparently evolved in order to achieve a higher degree of accuracy and speed in forward passing than would be obtained with a spherical ball, thus increasing the repeatability of an important phase of the game.

The rules of a football game, like laws, rituals, customs, and mores, are registered and preserved forms of sequential significances enabling people to share the significances of occurrences. The sharing of sequential significances which have value for us provides the links that operationally make social events possible. They are analogous to the forces of attraction that hold parts of an atom together, keeping each part from following its individual, independent course.

From this point of view it is inaccurate and misleading to say that different people have different "attitudes" concerning the same "thing." For the "thing" simply is not the same for different people whether the "thing" is a football game, a presidential candidate, Communism, or spinach. We do not simply "react to" a happening or to some impingement from the environment in a determined way (except in behavior that has become reflexive or habitual). We behave according to what we bring to the occasion, and what each of us brings to the occasion is more or less unique. And except for these significances which we bring to the occasion, the happenings around us would be meaningless occurrences, would be "inconsequential."

From the transactional view, an attitude is not a predisposition to react in a certain way to an occurrence or stimulus "out there" that exists in its own right with certain fixed characteristics which we "color" according to our predisposition. That is, a subject does not simply "react to" an "object." An attitude would rather seem to be a complex of registered significances reactivated by some stimulus which assumes its own particular significance for us in terms of our purposes. That is, the object as experienced would not exist for us except for the reactivated aspects of the form-world which provide particular significance to the hieroglyphics of sensory impingements.

Learn More About Confirmation Bias

See following link for a wonderfully entertaining podcast on the subject hosted by Dr. Todd Fleischer and Dr. Jerry Bockoven. Make sure you listen out for the poem entitled Food For Thought, sheer genius!

kitchenshrinks.com/2011/07/07/confirmation-bias---we-see-it-when-we-believe-it.aspx.

4. WHAT'S WITH THE PITCHFORK?

When you study psychology you quickly discover that the universal symbol for the discipline is the pitchfork shaped image like the one in the picture above. Now while this is great for short hand purposes i.e. drawing the symbol rather than having to spell out the word psychology in full, have you ever wondered about where the psychology symbol originates?

The Devil is Not in The Detail

One interesting but incorrect suggestion is that the psychology symbol is somehow related to the trident carried by the devil. The theory goes that because mental illness was historically seen as the work of the devil, psychology by association was considered diabolical; and in an irreverent display of defiance, psychologists adopted the trident pitchfork shape as their official symbol.

It's All Greek To Me

To discover the origin of the psychology symbol, you simply have to trace its etymology (word origin and sense development). The symbol for psychology represents the penultimate letter of the Greek alphabet, psi, which is also the first letter of the Greek word psuche, meaning mind or soul, from which the term psyche arose; which in turn gave us the name of the discipline psychology which is most commonly defined as study of the mind.

PSY'CHE, *n.* (si'ke.) [Gr. ψυχη, the soul.

Perhaps the devil is in the detail after all!

5. A POOR LIFE THIS

"*There's no advantage to hurrying through life.*"

(Masashi Kishimoto)

Here's a story that really made me think. "*In a banal setting at an inconvenient time, would beauty transcend?*"

Gene Weingarten, The Washington Post staff writer who ran the story described it as "*an experiment in context, perception and priorities - as well as an unblinking assessment of public taste*". The question at the heart of Weingarten's piece was whether one of the world's greatest musicians would be noticed in a D.C. Metro stop during rush hour? The musician in question was violinist Joshua Bell.

"*No one knew it, but the fiddler standing against a bare wall outside the Metro in an indoor arcade at the top of the escalators was one of the finest classical musicians in the world, playing some of the most elegant music ever written on one of the most valuable violins ever made.*"

In addition to asking his readers what he thought would happen, Weingarten also canvassed the opinion of Leonard Slatkin, music director of the National Symphony Orchestra - who stated "*Let's assume that he is not recognized and just taken for granted as a street musician . . . Still, I don't think that if he's really good, he's going to go unnoticed. He'd get a larger audience in Europe . . . but, okay, out of 1,000 people, my guess is there might be 35 or 40 who will recognize the quality for what it is. Maybe 75 to 100 will stop and spend some time listening.*"

So What Happened?

Joshua Bell played for three-quarters of an hour in which time 1,104 people went by. Of those people only seven stopped to listen for at least for a minute.

You can watch Joshua Bell's D.C Metro Performance via the following link.

www.youtube.com/watch?v=hnOPu0_YWhw

Slow Down, You Move Too Fast

Concern over the costs of our pace of life is just one of the issues raised by this engaging story, however, as this famous verse by William Henry Davies (first published in 1911) attests and as Weingarten alludes to in his article, it would be wrong to assume that this concern is something new.

What is this life if full of care

We have no time to stand and stare?

No time to stand beneath the boughs

And stare as long as sheep, or cows.

No time to see, when woods we pass,

Where squirrels hide their nuts in grass.

No time to see, in broad daylight,

Streams full of stars, like skies at night.

No time to turn at Beauty's glance,

And watch her feet, how they can dance.

No time to wait till her mouth can

Enrich that smile her eyes began.

A poor life this, if full of care,

We have no time to stand and stare.

I highly recommend reading Weingarten's article in full, which you can do so via the following link.

www.washingtonpost.com/wp-dyn/content/article/2007/04/04/AR2007040401721.html

6. FEAR

"The mark of fear is not easily removed."

(Ernest Gaines)

If the picture above sends a shiver down your spine then you are probably suffering from coulrophobia (fear of clowns.) According to Professor of psychology, Ronald M. Doctor (please let the M stand for McDonald!) fear of clowns may be associated with the human tendency - particularly among young children - to be "*very reactive to a familiar body type with an unfamiliar face.*"

A phobia is an acute, irrational fear of something which poses little or no real danger. According to the U.S National Institute of Mental Health (NIMH) specific phobias affect an estimated 19.2 million adult Americans and are twice as common in women as men. Many of the more common phobias people report are related to closed-in places, heights, escalators, tunnels, animals, water, flying and injuries involving blood.

The causes of specific phobias are not that well understood which is unsurprising given that they cover everything from **(A)**straphobia – *fear of thunder and lightning* - **To (Z)**oophobia – *fear of animals.* Indeed, such is the range of things that people report as the basis of a phobia when you hear about some of them you do so with almost a sense of disbelief.

Take a look at the following phobias. 12 are genuine; can you spot the 3 fictional phobias? I'll post the answer shortly.

1. Pinaciphobia – fear of lists

2. Chaetophobia – fear of hair

3. Arachibutyrophobia – fear of peanut butter sticking to the roof of the mouth.

4. Oikophobia – fear of household appliances

5. Neophobia - fear of new things

6. Hylophobia - fear of wood, forests, and trees

7. Aibohphobia - fear of palindromes

8. Decidophobia – fear of making decisions

9. Trypophobia – fear of clustered holes

10. Chronophobia – fear of time passing

11. Omphalophobia – fear of bellybuttons

12. Hippopotomonstrosesquipedaliophobia – fear of long words

13. Panphobia – fear of everything

14. Ablutophobia – fear of bathing, washing, or cleaning

15. Heliophobia – fear of sunlight

Phobias have long been a source of psychological interest, for instance, fear of the number thirteen (Triskaidekaphobia) can be traced back to 1911 when Isador Coriat referred to this particular phobia in his book on Abnormal Psychology.

Fear Not! Help is at Hand

Thanks to the pioneering work of South African psychiatrist, Joseph Wolpe there is a very effective treatment for phobias known as systematic desensitization. Drawing upon behaviorist principles of learning and "unconditioning," systematic desensitization is a therapeutic procedure which combines relaxation techniques alongside gradual exposure to the object of anxiety.

Wolpe described the procedure as follows:

"*The desensitization method consists of presenting to the imagination of the deeply relaxed patient the feeblest item in a list of anxiety-evoking stimuli - repeatedly, until no more anxiety is evoked. The next item of the list is then presented, and so on, until eventually even the strongest of the anxiety-evoking stimuli fails to evoke any stir of anxiety in the patient.*"

To learn more about Joseph Wolpe's revolutionary phobia treatment and its broader impact within the field of psychotherapy, see following link to listen to an excellent BBC radio broadcast on the subject presented by Claudia Hammond.

www.bbc.co.uk/programmes/b01g5yy1

Fictional Phobias

Well done if you went for:

3. Arachibutyrophobia – fear of peanut butter sticking to the roof of the mouth.

7. Aibohphobia - fear of palindromes (think about it!)

12. Hippopotomonstrosesquipedaliophobia – fear of long words

A Case Study in Fear

Fear was the subject one of the most (in)famous psychology studies ever conducted. Conditioned Emotional Reactions by John B. Watson and Rosalie Rayner attempted to show how fear could be induced in an infant through classical conditioning. The study became known forever as "The Case of Little Albert"

Originally published in 1920 and now in the public domain, Conditioned Emotional Reactions remains among the most frequently cited journal articles in introductory psychology courses and textbooks.

If you would like to read this iconic article in full, learn about little Albert's real identity and find out what happened to him, the rest of this chapter is for you.

Note To Students

If you ever have to do a paper, assignment or class project on little Albert, having access to Watson's and Rayner's original work in full will prove invaluable. A psychology classic is by definition a must read; however, most seminal texts within the discipline remain unread by a majority of psychology students. A detailed, well written description of a classic study is fine to a point, but there is absolutely no substitute for understanding and engaging with the issues under review than by reading the authors unabridged ideas, thoughts and findings in their entirety.

As a psychology student I achieved my best grades when I was able to draw upon relevant research articles in full. When establishing your position or structuring your arguments you simply have more opportunities to reflect and pick out salient points. Being able to read a classic article in full also allows you to pick out more subtle details and issues that can be overlooked. Speaking as somebody who has graded numerous papers submitted by students on the same topic, I can tell you that these more discerning observations stand out like a beacon in the dark!

Conditioned Emotional Reactions: The Case of Little Albert

In recent literature various speculations have been entered into concerning the possibility of conditioning various types of emotional response, but direct experimental evidence in support of such a view has been lacking. If the theory advanced by Watson and Morgan to the effect that in infancy the original emotional reaction patterns are few, consisting so far as observed of fear, rage and love, then there must be some simple method by means of which the range of stimuli which can call out these emotions and their compounds is greatly increased. Otherwise, complexity in adult response could not be accounted for. These authors without adequate experimental evidence advanced the view that this range was increased by means of conditioned reflex factors. It was suggested there that the early home life of the child furnishes a laboratory situation for establishing conditioned emotional responses. The present authors have recently put the whole matter to an experimental test.

Experimental work had been done so far on only one child, Albert B. This infant was reared almost from birth in a hospital environment; his mother was a wet nurse in the Harriet Lane Home for Invalid Children. Albert's life was normal: he was healthy from birth and one of the best developed youngsters ever brought to the hospital, weighing twenty-one pounds at nine months of age. He was on the whole stolid and unemotional. His stability was one of the principal reasons for using him as a subject in this test. We felt that we could do him relatively little harm by carrying out such experiments as those outlined below.

At approximately nine months of age we ran him through the emotional tests that have become a part of our regular routine in determining whether fear reactions can be called out by other stimuli than sharp noises and the sudden removal of support. Tests of this type have been described by the senior author in another place. In brief, the infant was confronted suddenly and for the first time successively with a white rat, a rabbit, a dog, a monkey, with masks with and without hair, cotton wool, burning newspapers, etc. A permanent record of Albert's reactions to these objects and situations has been preserved in a motion picture study. Manipulation was the most usual reaction called out. At no time did this infant ever show fear in any situation. These experimental records were confirmed by the casual observations of the mother and hospital attendants. No one had ever seen him in a state of fear and rage. The infant practically never cried.

Up to approximately nine months of age we had not tested him with loud sounds. The test to determine whether a fear reaction could be called out by a loud sound was made when he was eight months, twenty-six days of age. The sound was that made by striking a hammer upon a suspended steel bar four feet in length and three-fourths of an inch in diameter. The laboratory notes are as follows:

One of the two experimenters caused the child to turn its head and fixate her moving hand; the other stationed back of the child, struck the steel bar a sharp blow. The child started violently, his breathing was checked and the arms were raised in a characteristic manner. On the second stimulation the same thing occurred, and in addition the lips began to pucker and tremble. On the third stimulation the child broke into a sudden crying fit. This is the first time an emotional situation in the laboratory has produced any fear or even crying in Albert.

We had expected just these results on account of our work with other infants brought up under similar conditions. It is worthwhile to call attention to the fact that removal of support (dropping and jerking the blanket upon which the infant was lying) was tried exhaustively upon this infant on the same occasion. It was not effective in producing the fear response. This stimulus is effective in younger children. At what age such stimuli lose their potency in producing fear is not known. Nor is it known whether less placid children ever lose their fear of them. This probably depends upon the training the child gets. It is well known that children eagerly run to be tossed into the air and caught. On the other hand it is equally well known that in the adult fear responses are called out quite clearly by the sudden removal of support, if the individual is walking across a bridge, walking out upon a beam, etc. There is a wide field of study here which is aside from our present point.

The sound stimulus, thus, at nine months of age, gives us the means of testing several important factors.

I. Can we condition fear of an animal, e.g., a white rat, by visually presenting it and simultaneously striking a steel bar?

II. If such a conditioned emotional response can be established, will there be a transfer to other animals or other objects?

III. What is the effect of time upon such conditioned emotional responses?

IV. If after a reasonable period such emotional responses have not died out, what laboratory methods can be devised for their removal?

I. The establishment of conditioned emotional responses

At first there was considerable hesitation upon our part in making the attempt to set up fear reactions experimentally. A certain responsibility attaches to such a procedure. We decided finally to make the attempt, comforting ourselves by the reflection that such attachments would arise anyway as soon as the child left the sheltered environment of the nursery for the rough and tumble of the home. We did not begin this work until Albert was eleven months, three days of age. Before attempting to set up a conditioned response we, as before, put him through all of the regular emotional tests. Not the slightest sign of a fear response was obtained in any situation.

The steps taken to condition emotional responses are shown in our laboratory notes.

11 Months 3 Days

1. White rat suddenly taken from the basket and presented to Albert. He began to reach for rat with left hand. Just as his hand touched the animal the bar was struck immediately behind his head. The infant jumped violently and fell forward, burying his face in the mattress. He did not cry, however.

2. Just as the right hand touched the rat the bar was again struck. Again the infant jumped violently, fell forward and began to whimper.

In order not to disturb the child too seriously no further tests were given for one week.

11 Months 10 Days

1. Rat presented suddenly without sound. There was steady fixation but no tendency at first to reach for it. The rat was then placed nearer, whereupon tentative reaching movements began with the right hand. When the rat nosed the infant's left hand, the hand was immediately withdrawn. He started to reach for the head of the animal with the forefinger of the left hand, but withdrew it suddenly before contact. It is thus seen that the two joint stimulations given the previous week were not without effect. He was tested with his blocks immediately afterwards to see if they shared in the process of conditioning. He began immediately to pick them up, dropping them, pounding them, etc. In the remainder of the tests the blocks were given frequently to quiet him and to test his general emotional state. They were always removed from sight when the process of conditioning was under way.

2. Joint stimulation with rat and sound. Started, then fell over immediately to right side No crying.

2. Joint stimulation with rat and sound. Started, then fell over immediately to right side No crying.

2. Joint stimulation with rat and sound. Started, then fell over immediately to right side No crying.

5. Rat suddenly presented alone. Puckered face, whimpered and withdrew body sharply to the left.

6. Joint stimulation. Fell over immediately to right side and began to whimper.

7. Joint stimulation. Started violently and cried, but did not fall over.

8. Rat alone. The instant the rat was shown the baby began to cry. Almost instantly he turned sharply to the left, fell over on left side, raised himself on all fours and began to crawl away so rapidly that he was caught with difficulty before reaching the edge of the table.

This was as convincing a case of a completely conditioned fear response as could have been theoretically pictured. In all seven joint stimulations were given to bring about the complete reaction. It is not unlikely had the sound been of greater intensity or of a more complex clang character that the number of joint stimulations might have been materially reduced. Experiments designed to define the nature of the sounds that will serve best as emotional stimuli are under way.

II. When a conditioned emotional response has been established for one object, is there a transfer?

Five days later Albert was again brought back into the laboratory and tested as follows:

11 Months 15 Days

1. Tested first with blocks. He reached readily for them, playing with them as usual. This shows that there has been no general transfer to the room, table, blocks, etc.

2. Rat alone. Whimpered immediately, withdrew right hand and turned head and trunk away.

3. Blocks again offered. Played readily with them, smiling and gurgling.

4. Rat alone. Leaned over to the left side as far away from the rat as possible, then fell over, getting up on all fours and scurrying away as rapidly as possible.

5. Blocks again offered. Reached immediately for them, smiling and laughing as before.

The above preliminary test shows that the conditioned response to the rat had carried over completely for the five days in which no tests were given. The question as to whether or not there is a transfer was next taken up.

6. Rabbit alone. The rabbit was suddenly placed on the mattress in front of him. The reaction was pronounced. Negative responses began at once. He leaned as far away from the animal as possible, whimpered, then burst into tears. When the rabbit was placed in contact with him he buried his face in the mattress, then got up on all fours and crawled away, crying as he went. This was a most convincing test.

7. The blocks were next given him, after an interval. He played with them as before. It was observed by four people that he played far more energetically with them than ever before. The blocks were raised high over his head and slammed down with a great deal of force.

8. Dog alone. The dog did not produce as violent a reaction as the rabbit. The moment fixation occurred the child shrank back and as the animal came nearer he attempted to get on all fours but did not cry at first. As soon as the dog passed out of his range of vision he became quiet. The dog was then made to approach the infant's head (he was lying down at the moment). Albert straightened up immediately, fell over to the opposite side and turned his head away. He then began to cry.

9. The blocks were again presented. He began immediately to play with them.

10. Fur coat (seal). Withdrew immediately to the left side and began to fret. Coat put close to him on the left side, he turned immediately, began to cry and tried to crawl away on all fours.

11. Cotton wool. The wool was presented in a paper package. At the end the cotton was not covered by the paper. It was placed first on his feet. He kicked it away but did not touch it with his hands. When his hand was laid on the wool he immediately withdrew it but did not show the shock that the animals or fur coat produced in him. He then began to play with the paper, avoiding contact with the wool itself. He finally, under the impulse of the manipulative instinct, lost some of his negativism to the wool.

12. Just in play W. put his head down to see if Albert would play with his hair. Albert was completely negative. Two other observers did the same thing. He began immediately to play with their hair. W. then brought the Santa Claus mask and presented it to Albert. He was again pronouncedly negative.

11 Months 20 Days

1. Blocks alone. Played with them as usual.

2. Rat alone. Withdrawal of the whole body, bending over to left side, no crying. Fixation and following with eyes. The response was much less marked than on first presentation the previous week. It was thought best to freshen up the reaction by another joint stimulation.

3. Just as the rat was placed on his hand the rod was struck. Reaction violent.

4. Rat alone. Fell over at once to left side. Reaction practically as strong as on former occasion but no crying.

5. Rat alone. Fell over to left side, got up on all fours and started to crawl away. On this occasion there was no crying, but strange to say, as he started away he began to gurgle and coo, even while leaning far over to the left side to avoid the rat.

6. Rabbit alone. Leaned over to left side as far as possible. Did not fall over. Began to whimper but reaction not so violent as on former occasions.

7. Blocks again offered. He reached for them immediately and began to play.

All of these tests so far discussed were carried out upon a table supplied with a mattress, located in a small, well-lighted dark-room. We wished to test next whether conditioned fear responses so set up would appear if the situation were markedly altered. We thought it best before making this test to freshen the reaction both to the rabbit and to the dog by showing them at the moment the steel bar was struck. It will be recalled that this was the first time any effort had been made to directly condition response to the dog and rabbit. The experimental notes are as follows:

8. The rabbit at first was given alone. The reaction was exactly as given in test (6) above. When the rabbit was left on Albert's knees for a long time he began tentatively to reach out and manipulate its fur with forefingers. While doing this the steel rod was struck. A violent fear reaction resulted.

9. Rabbit alone. Reaction wholly similar to that on trial (6) above.

10. Rabbit alone. Started immediately to whimper, holding hands far up, but did not cry. Conflicting tendency to manipulate very evident.

11. Dog alone. Began to whimper, shaking head from side to side, holding hands as far away from the animal as possible.

12. Dog and sound. The rod was struck just as the animal touched him. A violent negative reaction appeared. He began to whimper, turned to one side, fell over and started to get up on all fours.

13. Blocks. Played with them immediately and readily.

On this same day and immediately after the above experiment Albert was taken into the large well-lighted lecture room belonging to the laboratory. He was placed on a table in the center of the room immediately under the skylight. Four people were present. The situation was thus very different from that which obtained in the small dark room.

1. Rat alone. No sudden fear reaction appeared at first. The hands, however, were held up and away from the animal. No positive manipulatory reactions appeared.

2. Rabbit alone. Fear reaction slight. Turned to left and kept face away from the animal but the reaction was never pronounced.

3. Dog alone. Turned away but did not fall over. Cried. Hands moved as far away from the animal as possible. Whimpered as long as the dog was present.

4. Rat alone. Slight negative reaction.

5. Rat and sound. It was thought best to freshen the reaction to the rat. The sound was given just as the rat was presented. Albert jumped violently but did not cry.

6. Rat alone. At first he did not show any negative reaction. When rat was placed nearer he began to show negative reaction by drawing back his body, raising his hands, whimpering, etc.

7. Blocks. Played with them immediately.

8. Rat alone. Pronounced withdrawal of body and whimpering.

9. Blocks. Played with them as before.

10. Rabbit alone. Pronounced reaction. Whimpered with arms held high, fell over backward and had to be caught.

11. Dog alone. At first the dog did not produce the pronounced reaction. The hands were held high over the head, breathing was checked, but there was no crying. Just at this moment the dog, which had not barked before, barked three times loudly when only about six inches from the baby's face. Albert immediately fell over and broke into a wail that continued until the dog was removed. The sudden barking of the hitherto quiet dog produced a marked fear response in the adult observers!

From the above results it would seem that emotional transfers do take place. Furthermore it would seem that the number of transfers resulting from an experimentally produced conditioned emotional reaction may be very large. In our observations we had no means of testing the complete number of transfers which may have resulted.

III. The effect of time upon conditioned emotional responses

We have already shown that the conditioned emotional response will continue for a period of one week. It was desired to make the time test longer. In view of the imminence of Albert's departure from the hospital we could not make the interval longer than one month Accordingly no further emotional experimentation was entered into for thirty-one days after the above test. During the month, however, Albert was brought weekly to the laboratory for tests upon right and left-handedness, imitation, general development, etc. No emotional tests whatever were given and during the whole month his regular nursery routine was maintained in the Harriet Lane Home. The notes on the test given at the end of this period are as follows:

1 Year 21 Days

1. Santa Claus mask. Withdrawal, gurgling, then slapped at it without touching. When his hand was forced to touch it, he whimpered and cried. His hand was forced to touch it two more times. He whimpered and cried on both tests. He finally cried at the mere visual stimulus of the mask.

2. Fur coat. Wrinkled his nose and withdrew both hands, drew back his whole body and began to whimper as the coat was put nearer. Again there was the strife between withdrawal and the tendency to manipulate. Reached tentatively with left hand but drew back before contact had been made. In moving his body to one side his hand accidentally touched the coat. He began to cry at once, nodding his head in a very peculiar manner (this reaction was an entirely new one). Both hands were withdrawn as far as possible from the coat. The coat was then laid on his lap and he continued nodding his head and whimpering, withdrawing his body as far as possible, pushing the while at the coat with his feet but never touching it with his hands.

3. Fur coat. The coat was taken out of his sight and presented again at the end of a minute. He began immediately to fret, withdrawing his body and nodding his head as before.

4. Blocks. He began to play with them as usual.

5. The rat. He allowed the rat to crawl towards him without withdrawing. He sat very still and fixated it intently. Rat then touched his hand. Albert withdrew it immediately, then leaned back as far as possible but did not cry. When the rat was placed on his arm he withdrew his body and began to fret, nodding his head. The rat was then allowed to crawl against his chest. He first began to fret and then covered his eyes with both hands.

6. Blocks. Reaction normal.

7. The rabbit. The animal was placed directly in front of him. It was very quiet. Albert showed no avoiding reactions at first. After a few seconds he puckered up his face, began to nod his head and to look intently at the experimenter. He next began to push the rabbit away with his feet, withdrawing his body at the same time. Then as the rabbit came nearer he began pulling his feet away, nodding his head, and wailing "da da". After about a minute he reached out tentatively and slowly and touched the rabbit's ear with his right hand, finally manipulating it. The rabbit was again placed in his lap. Again he began to fret and withdrew his hands. He reached out tentatively with his left hand and touched the animal, shuddered and withdrew the whole body. The experimenter then took hold of his left hand and laid it on the rabbit's back. Albert immediately withdrew his hand and began to suck his thumb. Again the rabbit was laid in his lap. He began to cry, covering his face with both hands.

8. Dog. The dog was very active. Albert fixated it intensely for a few seconds, sitting very still. He began to cry but did not fall over backwards as on his last contact with the dog. When the dog was pushed closer to him he at first sat motionless, then began to cry, putting both hands over his face.

These experiments would seem to show conclusively that directly conditioned emotional responses as well as those conditioned by transfer persist, although with a certain loss in the intensity of the reaction, for a longer period than one month. Our view is that they persist and modify personality throughout life. It should be recalled again that Albert was of an extremely phlegmatic type. Had he been emotionally unstable probably both the directly conditioned response and those transferred would have persisted throughout the month unchanged in form.

IV. "Detachment" or removal of conditioned emotional responses

Unfortunately Albert was taken from the hospital the day the above tests were made. Hence the opportunity of building up an experimental technique by means of which we could remove the conditioned emotional responses was denied us. Our own view, expressed above, which is possibly not very well grounded, is that these responses in the home environment are likely to persist indefinitely, unless an accidental method for removing them is hit upon. The importance of establishing some method must be apparent to all. Had the opportunity been at hand we should have tried out several methods, some of which we may mention. (I) Constantly confronting the child with those stimuli which called out the responses in the hopes that habituation would come in corresponding to "fatigue" of reflex when differential reactions are to be set up. (2) By trying to "recondition" by showing objects calling out fear responses (visual) and simultaneously stimulating the erogenous zones (tactual). We should try first the lips, then the nipples and as a final resort the sex organs. (3) By trying to "recondition" by feeding the subject candy or other food just as the animal is shown. This method calls for the food control of the subject. (4) By building up "constructive" activities around the object by imitation and by putting the hand through the motions of manipulation. At this age imitation of overt motor activity is strong, as our present but unpublished experimentation has shown.

INCIDENTAL OBSERVATIONS

(a) Thumb sucking as a compensatory device for blocking fear and noxious stimuli. During the course of these experiments, especially in the final test, it was noticed that whenever Albert was on the verge of tears or emotionally upset generally he would continually thrust his thumb into his mouth. The moment the hand reached the mouth he became impervious to the stimuli producing fear. Again and again while the motion pictures were being made at the end of the thirty-day period, we had to remove the thumb from his mouth before the conditioned response could be obtained. This method of blocking noxious and emotional stimuli (fear and rage) through erogenous stimulation seems to persist from birth onward. Very often in our experiments upon the work adders with infants under ten days of age the same reaction appeared. When at work upon the adders both of the infants arms are under slight restraint. Often rage appears. They begin to cry, thrashing their arms and legs about. If the finger gets into the mouth crying ceases at once. The organism thus apparently from birth, when under the influence of love stimuli is blocked to all others. This resort to sex stimulation when under the influence of noxious and emotional situations, or when the individual is restless and idle, persists throughout adolescent and adult life. Albert, at any rate, did not resort to thumb sucking except in the presence of such stimuli. Thumb sucking could immediately be checked by offering him his blocks. These invariably called out active manipulation instincts. It is worth while here to call attention to the fact that Freud's conception of the stimulation of erogenous zones as being the expression of an original "pleasure" seeking principle may be turned about and possibly better described as a compensatory (and often conditioned) device for the blockage of noxious and fear and rage producing stimuli.

(b) Equal primacy of fear, love and possibly rage. While in general the results of our experiment offer no particular points of conflict with Freudian concepts, one fact out of harmony with them should be emphasized. According to proper Freudians sex (or in our terminology, love) is the principal emotion in which conditioned responses arise which later limit and distort personality. We wish to take sharp issue with this view on the basis of the experimental evidence we have gathered. Fear is as primal a factor as love in influencing personality. Fear does not gather its potency in any derived manner from love. It belongs to the original and inherited nature of man. Probably the same may be true of rage although at present we are not so sure of this.

The Freudians twenty years from now, unless their hypotheses change, when they come to analyze Albert's fear of a seal skin coat - assuming that he comes to analysis at that age - will probably tease from him the recital of a dream which upon their analysis will show that Albert at three years of age attempted to play with the pubic hair of the mother and was scolded violently for it. (We are by no means denying that this might in some other case condition it). If the analyst has sufficiently prepared Albert to accept such a dream when found as an explanation of his avoiding tendencies, and if the analyst has the authority and personality to put it over, Albert may be fully convinced that the dream was a true revealer of the factors which brought about the fear.

It is probable that many of the phobias in psychopathology are true conditioned emotional reactions either of the direct or the transferred type. One may possibly have to believe that such persistence of early conditioned responses will be found only in persons who are constitutionally inferior. Our argument is meant to be constructive. Emotional disturbances in adults cannot be traced back to sex alone. They must be retraced along at least three collateral lines - to conditioned and transferred responses set up in infancy and early youth in all three of the fundamental human emotions.

Bonus Material

One of the most dramatic aspects of Watson and Rayner's original study was that they had planned to test a number of methods by which they could remove Little Albert's conditioned fear responses. However, as was noted "*Unfortunately Albert was taken from the hospital the day the above tests were made. Hence the opportunity of building up an experimental technique by means of which we could remove the conditioned emotional responses was denied us."*

This unfortunate turn of events was something that obviously stayed with Watson, as under his guidance some three years later, Mary Cover Jones conducted a follow-up study which illustrated how fear could be removed under laboratory conditions. This additional and highly relevant article is also presented in full below.

A Laboratory Study of Fear: The Case of Peter

As part of a genetic study of emotions, a number of children were observed in order to determine the most effective methods of removing fear responses.

The case of Peter illustrates how a fear may be removed under laboratory conditions. His case was selected from a number of others for the following reasons:

1. Progress in combating the fear reactions was so marked that many of the details of the process could be observed easily.

2. It was possible to continue the study over a period of more than three months.

3. The notes of a running diary show the characteristics of a healthy, normal, interesting child, well adjusted, except for his exaggerated fear reactions. A few descriptive notes show something of his personality:

Remarkably active, easily interested, capable of prolonged endeavor...A favorite with the children as well as with the nurses and matrons...Peter has a healthy passion for possessions. Everything that he lays his hands on is his. As this is frequently disputed by some other child, there are occasional violent scenes of protest. These disturbances are not more frequent than might be expected in a three-year-old, in view of the fact that he is continually forced to adjust to a large group of children, nor are they more marked in Peter's case than in others of his age. Peter's I.Q. at the age of 2 years and 10 months was 102 on the Kuhlmann Revision of the Binet. At the same time he passed 5 of the 3 year tests on the Stanford Revision. In initiative and constructive ability, however, he is superior to his companions of the same mental age.

4. The case is a sequel to one recently contributed by Dr. Watson and furnished supplementary material of interest in a genetic study of emotions. Dr. Watson's case illustrated how a fear could be produced experimentally under laboratory conditions. A brief review follows: Albert, eleven months of age, was an infant with a phlegmatic disposition, afraid of nothing "under the sun" except a loud sound made by striking a steel bar. This made him cry. By striking the bar at the same time that Albert touched a white rat, the fear was transferred to the white rat. After seven combined stimulations, rat and sound, Albert not only became greatly disturbed at the sight of a rat, but this fear had spread to include a white rabbit, cotton wool, a fur coat, and the experimenter's hair. It did not transfer to his wooden blocks and other objects very dissimilar to the rat.

In referring to this case, Dr. Watson says, "We have shown experimentally that when you condition a child to show fear of an animal, this fear transfers or spreads in such a way that without separate conditioning he becomes afraid of many animals. If you take any one of these objects producing fear and uncondition, will fear of the other objects in the series disappear at the same time? That is, will the unconditioning spread without further training to other stimuli?"

Dr. Watson intended to continue the study of Albert in an attempt to answer this question, but Albert was removed from the hospital and the series of observations was discontinued.

About three years later this case, which seemed almost to be Albert grown a bit older, was discovered in our laboratory.

Peter was 2 years and 10 months old when we began to study him. He was afraid of a white rat, and this fear extended to a rabbit, a fur coat, a feather, cotton wool, etc., but not to wooden blocks and similar toys. An abridgment of the first laboratory notes on Peter reads as follows:

Peter was put in a crib in a play room and immediately became absorbed in his toys. A white rat was introduced into the crib from behind. (The experimenter was behind a screen). At sight of the rat, Peter screamed and fell flat on his back in a paroxysm of fear. The stimulus was removed, and Peter was taken out of the crib and put into a chair. Barbara was brought to the crib and the white rat introduced as before. She exhibited no fear but picked the rat up in her hand. Peter sat quietly watching Barbara and the rat. A string of beads belonging to Peter had been left in the crib. Whenever the rat touched a part of the string he would say "my beads" in a complaining voice, although he made no objections when Barbara touched them. Invited to get down from the chair, he shook his head, fear not yet subsided. Twenty-five minutes elapsed before he was ready to play about freely.

The next day his reactions to the following situations and objects were noted:

Play room and crib: Selected toys, got into crib without protest.

White ball rolled in: Picked it up and held it.

Fur rug hung over crib: Cried until it was removed.

Fur coat hung over crib: Cried until it was removed.

Cotton: Whimpered, withdrew, cried.

Hat with feathers: Cried.

Blue woolly sweater: Looked, turned away, no fear.

White toy rabbit of rough cloth: No interest, no fear.

Wooden doll: No interest, no fear.

This case made it possible for the experiment to continue where Dr. Watson had left off. The first problem was that of "unconditioning" a fear response to an animal, and the second, that of determining whether unconditioning to one stimulus spreads without further training to other stimuli.

From the test situations which were used to reveal fears, it was found that Peter showed even more marked fear responses to the rabbit than to the rat. It was decided to use the rabbit for unconditioning and to proceed as follows: Each day Peter and three other children were brought to the laboratory for a play period. The other children were selected carefully because of their entirely fearless attitude toward the rabbit and because of their satisfactory adjustments in general. The rabbit was always present during a part of the play period. From to time Peter was brought in alone so that his reactions could be observed and progress noted.

From reading over the notes for each session it was apparent that there had been improvement by more or less regular steps from almost complete terror at sight of the rabbit to a completely positive response with no signs of disturbance. New situations requiring closer contact with the rabbit had been gradually introduced and the degree to which these situations were avoided, tolerated, or welcomed, at each experimental session, gave the measure of improvement. Analysis of the notes on Peter's reactions indicated the following progressive steps in his degrees of toleration:

A. Rabbit anywhere in the room in a cage causes fear reactions.

B. Rabbit 12 feet away in cage tolerated.

C. Rabbit 4 feet away in cage tolerated.

D. Rabbit 3 feet away in cage tolerated.

E. Rabbit close in cage tolerated.

F. Rabbit free in cage tolerated.

G. Rabbit touched when experimenter holds it.

H. Rabbit touched when free in room.

I. Rabbit defied by spitting at it, throwing things at it, imitating it.

J. Rabbit allowed on tray of high chair.

K. Squats in defenseless position beside rabbit.

L. Helps experimenter to carry rabbit to its cage.

M. Holds rabbit on lap.

N. Stays alone in room with rabbit.

O. Allows rabbit in play pen with him.

P. Fondles rabbit affectionately.

Q. Lets rabbit nibble his fingers.

These "degrees of toleration" merely represented the stages in which improvement occurred. They did not give any indications of the intervals between steps, nor of the plateaus, relapses, and sudden gains which were actually evident.

To show these features a curve was drawn by using the seventeen steps given above as the Y axis of a chart and the experimental sessions as the X axis. The units are not equal on either axis, as the "degrees of toleration" were merely set down as they appeared from consideration of the laboratory notes with no attempt to evaluate the steps. Likewise the experimental sessions were not equidistant in time. Peter was seen twice daily for a period and thence only once a day. At one point illness and quarantine interrupted the experiments for two months.

The question arose as to whether or not the points on the Y axis which indicated progress to the experimenter represented real advance and not merely idiosyncratic reactions of the subject. The "tolerance series" as indicated by the experimenter was presented in random order to six graduate students and instructors in psychology to be arranged so as to indicate increase in tolerance, in their judgment. An average correlation of .70 with the experimenter's arrangement was found for the six ratings. This indicates that the experimenter was justified from an a priori point of view in designating the steps to be progressive stages. The first seven periods showed how Peter progressed from a great fear of the rabbit to a tranquil indifference and even a voluntary pat on the rabbit's back when others were setting the example. The notes for the seventh period read:

Laurel, Mary, Arthur, Peter playing together in the laboratory. Experimenter put rabbit down on floor. Arthur said, "Peter doesn't cry when he sees the rabbit come out." Peter, "No." He was a little concerned as to whether or not the rabbit would eat his kiddie car. Laurel and Mary stroked the rabbit and chattered away excitedly. Peter walked over, touched the rabbit on the back, exulting, "I touched him on the end."

At this period Peter was taken to the hospital with scarlet fever. He did not return for two months. It was noted that there was a decided drop to the early level of fear reaction when he returned. This was easily explained by the nurse who brought Peter from the hospital. As they were entering a taxi at the door of the hospital, a large dog, running past, jumped at them. Both Peter and the nurse were very much frightened, Peter so much that he lay in the taxi pale and quiet, and the nurse debated whether or not to return him to the hospital. This seemed reason enough for his precipitate descent back to the original fear level. Being threatened by a large dog when ill, and in a strange place and being with an adult who also showed fear, was a terrifying situation against which our training could not have fortified him.

At this point we began another method of treatment, that of "direct conditioning." Peter was seated in a high chair and given food which he liked. The experimenter brought the rabbit in a wire cage as close as she could without arousing a response which would interfere with the eating.

Through the presence of the pleasant stimulus (food) whenever the rabbit was shown, the fear was eliminated gradually in favor of a positive response. Occasionally also, other children were brought in to help with the "unconditioning." These facts are of interest in following the charted progress. The first decided rise at (c) was due to the presence of another child who influenced Peter's reaction. The notes for this day read:

Lawrence and Peter sitting near together in their high chairs eating candy. Rabbit in cage put down 12 feet away. Peter began to cry. Lawrence said, "Oh, rabbit." Clambered down, ran over and looked in the cage at him. Peter followed close and watched.

The next two decided rises occurred on the day when a student assistant, Dr. S., was present. Peter was very fond of Dr. S. whom he insisted was his "papa." Although Dr. S. did not directly influence Peter by any overt suggestions, it may be that having him there contributed to Peter's general feeling of well being and thus indirectly affected his reactions. The fourth rise was, like the first, due to the influence of another child. Notes for the 21st session read:

Peter with candy in high chair. Experimenter brought rabbit and sat down in front of the tray with it. Peter cried out, "I don't want him," and withdrew. Rabbit was given to another child sitting near to hold. His holding the rabbit served as a powerful suggestion; Peter wanted the rabbit on his lap, and held it for an instant.

Another decided drop was caused by a slight scratch when Peter was helping to carry the rabbit to his cage. The rapid ascent following shows how quickly he regained lost ground.

In one of our last sessions, Peter showed no fear although another child was present who showed marked disturbance at sight of the rabbit.

An attempt was made from time to time to see what verbal organization accompanied this process of "unconditioning." Upon Peter's return from the hospital, the following conversation took place:

Experimenter: What do you do upstairs, Peter? (The laboratory was upstairs).

Peter: I see my brother. Take me up to see my brother.

Experimenter: What else will you see?

Peter: Blocks.

Peter's reference to blocks indicated a definite memory as he played with blocks only in the laboratory. No further response of any significance could be elicited. In the laboratory two days later (he had seen the rabbit once in the meantime), he said suddenly, "Beads can't bite me, beads can only look at me." Toward the end of the training an occasional "I like the rabbit," was all the language he had to parallel the changed emotional organization.

Early in the experiment an attempt was made to get some measure of the visceral changes accompanying Peter's fear reactions. On one occasion Dr. S. determined Peter's blood pressure outside the laboratory and again later, in the laboratory while he was in a state of much anxiety caused by the rabbit's being held close to him by the experimenter. The diastolic blood pressure changed from 65 to 80 on this occasion. Peter was taken to the infirmary the next day for the routine physical examination and developed there a suspicion of medical instruments which made it inadvisable to proceed with this phase of the work.

Peter has gone home to a difficult environment but the experimenter is still in touch with him. He showed in the last interview, as on the later portions of the chart, a genuine fondness for the rabbit. What has happened to the fear of the other objects? The fear of the cotton, the fur coat, feathers, was entirely absent at our last interview. He looked at them, handled them, and immediately turned to something which interested him more. The reaction to the rats, and the fur rug with the stuffed head was greatly modified and improved. While he did not show the fondness for these that was apparent with the rabbit, he had made a fair adjustment. For example, Peter would pick up the tin box containing frogs or rats and carry it around the room. When requested, he picked up the fur rug and carried it to the experimenter.

What would Peter do if confronted by a strange animal? At the last interview the experimenter presented a mouse and a tangled mass of angleworms. At first sight, Peter showed slight distress reactions and moved away, but before the period was over he was carrying the worms about and watching the mouse with undisturbed interest. By "unconditioning" Peter to the rabbit, he has apparently been helped to overcome many superfluous fears, some completely, some to a less degree. His tolerance of strange animals and unfamiliar situations has apparently increased.

The study is still incomplete. Peter's fear of the animals which were shown him was probably not a directly conditioned fear. It is unlikely that he had ever had any experience with white rats, for example. Where the fear originated and with what stimulus, is not known. Nor is it known what Peter would do if he were again confronted with the original fear situation. All of the fears which were "unconditioned" were transferred fears, and it has not yet been learned whether or not the primary fear can be eliminated by training the transfers.

Another matter which must be left to speculation is the future welfare of the subject. His "home" consists of one furnished room which is occupied by his mother and father, a brother of nine years and himself. Since the death of an older sister, he is the recipient of most of the unwise affection of his parents. His brother appears to bear him a grudge because of this favoritism, as might be expected. Peter hears continually, "Ben is so bad and so dumb, but Peter is so good and so smart!" His mother is a highly emotional individual who cannot get through an interview, however brief, without a display of tears. She is totally incapable of providing a home on the $25 a week which her husband steadily earns. In an attempt to control Peter she resorts to frequent fear suggestions. "Come in Peter, someone wants to steal you." To her erratic resorts to discipline, Peter reacts with temper tantrums. He was denied a summer in the country because his father "forgets he's tired when he has Peter around." Surely a discouraging outlook for Peter.

But the recent development of psychological studies of young children and the growing tendency to carry the knowledge gained in the psychological laboratories into the home and school induce us to predict a more wholesome treatment of a future generation of Peters.

Little Albert: A Mystery Solved?

For nearly a century little Albert's real identity and the question of what became of him remained unknown. However, thanks to the painstaking research efforts of psychology professors Hall P. Beck and Sharman Levinson the enduring mystery surrounding the most famous research subject in the history of psychology looks like it may have been finally solved. In 2009 Beck and Levinson published their findings in the journal, American Psychologist. (Beck, H.P., Levinson, S., Irons, G. (2009). Finding little Albert. A journey to John B. Watson's laboratory. American Psychologist, 64, 605-614.)

In summarizing what they discovered and how the authors noted "*Examinations of Watson's personal correspondence, scientific production (books, journal articles, film), and public documents (national census data, state birth and death records) suggested that an employee at the Harriet Lane Home was Albert's mother. Contact with the woman's descendents led the authors to the individual they believe to be 'Little Albert.'*"

That individual was Douglas Merritte whose mother Arvilla worked and lived on the Johns Hopkins campus where the little Albert experiment took place. This along with other compelling evidence presented by Beck, Levinson and Merritte family descendent Gary Irons "*strongly supports the hypothesis that Douglas Merritte is Little Albert.*"

Douglas, Son of Arvilla Merritte, March 9, 1919 to May 10, 1925

Tragically, Douglas developed hydrocephalus (a build-up of fluid on the brain) and died aged just 6 years old. Hall Beck's dream that one day he would be showing "Big Albert" Watson's film of him as a baby would never be realized.

"Our search of seven years was longer than the little boy's life. I laid flowers on the grave of my longtime "companion," turned, and simultaneously felt a great peace and profound loneliness."

7. GOOSEBUMPS, EARWORMS AND THE POWER OF MUSIC

"One good thing about music, when it hits you, you feel no pain."

(Bob Marley)

There are lots of fascinating types of psychology but the psychology of music rocks!

According to Richard Parncutt, Professor of Systematic Musicology at the University of Graz, music psychology investigates why humans spend so much time, effort and money on musical activities. This investigation combines the academic study of music (musicology) with the academic study of human individuals (psychology). Areas of psychology frequently drawn upon within the psychology of music include biopsychology, perception, cognition, creativity, motivation and emotion.

Professor Parncutt notes that the topic areas explored by music psychologists include, music rituals and gatherings, skills and processes Involved in learning a musical instrument, the role of music in forming personal and group identities, everyday music listening and responding emotionally to music.

And it is research into the last two topics (everyday music listening and responding emotionally to music) which have highlighted some incredibly interesting things that we can all relate to.

I Got Chills They're Multiplying!

I'm sure like most people you will have experienced that amazing buzz when listening to a particular song or piece of music? A tune so good or emotionally arousing, that it gives you goosebumps and makes your hair stand on end. Well, it turns out that these musical frissons like other happiness inducing experiences (sex, drugs, and food) are as a result of a dopamine rush.

Dopamine is a chemical neurotransmitter that helps regulate the reward and pleasure centers in the brain. A reinforcement and motivation stimulus, dopamine plays a very important role in our biological survival. Strikingly, therefore, given that music listening is not essential for human survival; dopamine release in this context serves to demonstrate the remarkable human ability to derive pleasure from abstract concepts such as music and art.

So What Does it For You?

What's your musical frisson number one? Which song or piece of music gives you goosebumps? Here are some of the replies I received when I asked this question on facebook.

Clare Island - The Saw Doctors.

Vivaldi - L' Olimpiade (Sinfonia Allegro) in facsimile.

You and your friend - Dire Straits.

Eulogy - Tool

Pavarotti - Nessun Dorma.

Simon And Garfunkel - The Sound of Silence.

Never let me go - Florence and The Machine.

The tune that does it for me is Bizarre Love Triangle by New Order. The 1980's was my decade and this anthem transports me straight back there every time, in fact I've got Frissons right now just thinking about it.

The Psychology Of Tunes That Stick In Our Heads

"You're suffering from a condition known as "Earworm..." when your brain becomes stuck on a catchy tune." (SpongeBob Square Pants: Season 8, episode 9, 2010)

Another very common musical experience is when a tune suddenly pops into your head and keeps on doing so over and over again. This phenomenon has been variously labeled - *tune in the brain syndrome, sticky music, cognitive itch, involuntary musical imagery* and my personal favorite "*earworms.*"

To find out just how common earworms are, Dr. Lassi A. Liikkanen from Aalto University in Finland conducted the first comprehensive study on the subject. Over 12,000 people completed an online survey, with 91% of respondents reporting experiencing earworms at least once a week.

In a quest to learn more about the music in people's heads, Dr Victoria Williamson and colleagues from Goldsmiths, University of London, are conducting collaborative research with BBC 6Music and the British Academy. One illuminating area of enquiry has been to explore the circumstances preceding an earworm episode. Among the triggers which can apparently cause a tune to pop into your head and become an earworm are:

Recent Exposure: A tune you recently heard becomes an earworm.

Repeated Exposure: A tune you heard on multiple occasions becomes an earworm.

Person Association: The earworm tune is linked to a person you have seen, talked or thought about.

Situation Association: The earworm tune is triggered by the situation or environment you find yourself in e.g., a wedding reminds you of your favorite love song.

Word Association: The earworm tune title or lyrics are linked to a word or words that you have seen or heard.

Mood State: The earworm tune is linked to your mood.

Stress State: The earworm tune is linked to your experience of an anxious or traumatic event.

Dream Recall: The earworm tune is connected to events you dreamt about.

Other interesting patterns found among those reporting earworms are that:

Women get earworms more than men.

The average length of an earworm is 27 minutes but for some people they can last for hours, days and even weeks.

Why Studying Earworms is Important

"*By learning about earworms we can understand more about: 1) how our involuntary memory systems work in both positive (creativity) and negative (rumination and PTSD) ways; and 2) how we can learn to use memory more effectively, for example using music to help children learn more effortlessly or aid those who are suffering from memory problems.*" (Dr Victoria Williamson)

The Earworm Project

If you are among the 90% of people who experience an earworm at least once a week, the Music, Mind and Brain group at Goldsmiths University would love to hear from you. See following link to find out more.

earwormery.com

Additional Information Links

Keep up-to-date with all the latest earworm research findings published by the Music, Mind and Brain group at Goldsmiths University.

www.gold.ac.uk/music-mind-brain/earworm-project

Dr Victoria Williamson's Music Psychology Blog is an outstanding resource for anybody interested in learning more about music psychology.

musicpsychology.co.uk

I would like to finish this chapter by acknowledging the incredible power of music and I can't think of a better way of doing this than by drawing your attention to - *Alive Inside: A Story of Music and Memory* by Michael Rossato-Bennett. This profoundly moving documentary chronicles social worker Dan Cohen's discovery that personalized music can awaken memories in people with Alzheimer's and dementia.

Meet Henry

During the making of the documentary a clip of Henry a 94 year old man with dementia was posted on YouTube. The clip went viral and within a week 7 million people had seen it. If you can, watch the clip right now via the following link.

youtu.be/fyZQf0p73QM

Just amazing! When you watch something like that it can be hard to find the words to do it justice, so I won't try; rather I'll leave you with an eloquent quote from renowned neurologist Dr. Oliver Sacks who features in the documentary.

"Music can lift us out of depression or move us to tears - it is a remedy, a tonic, orange juice for the ear. But for many of my neurological patients, music is even more - it can provide access, even when no medication can, to movement, to speech, to life. For them, music is not a luxury, but a necessity."

Additional Information Links

See following link to learn more about the *Alive Inside* documentary film and the associated Music and Memory project designed to bring personalized music into the lives of the elderly or infirm.

www.ximotionmedia.com

Note To Psychology Students

The use of therapeutic music in a formalized setting would be a great topic for a research project or final year thesis/dissertation. Not least because Nina S. Parikh, PhD, from the Brookdale Center for Healthy Aging of Hunter College, CUNY has put together an extensive reference list of the latest research on the subject. You can access the reference list via the Music and Memory website - see following link.

musicandmemory.org/music-brain-resources/current-research

"Music has great lessons to teach us about what it means to be human."

(Michael Rossato-Bennet)

8. YOU'VE GOT TO FACE IT

"I never forget a face, but in your case I'll be glad to make an exception."

(Groucho Marx)

Face perception is a very important human attribute. Our brains it would seem are hard-wired to help us recognize the presence of a face from birth; newborn babies for instance will automatically focus attention towards any face-like pattern.

This deep-rooted face detection system remains operational throughout our lives. Let's see if we can trigger yours!

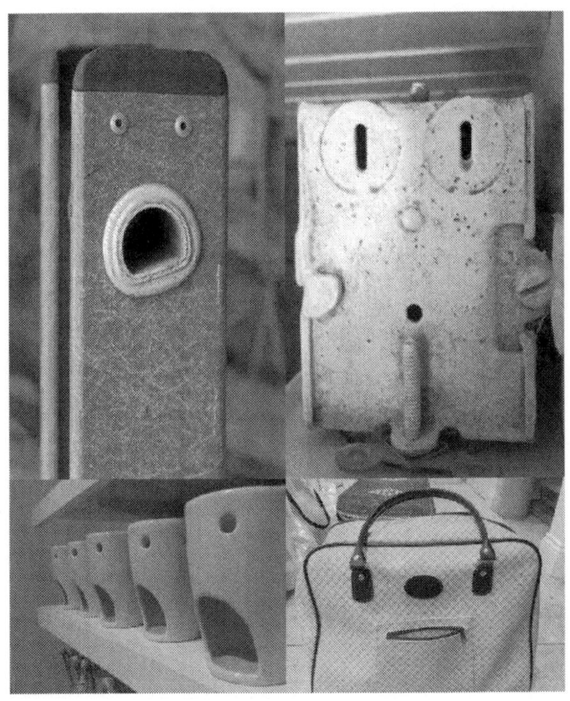

(Images courtesy of nottsexminer, thentoff & Nico via flickr)

See a face or two? Assuming you did, the psychological phenomenon you are experiencing is known as pareidolia i.e. the perception of an ambiguous and random stimulus as significant. One of the best known examples of pareidolia is the "face on Mars", the famous NASA image taken in 1976 by the Viking 1 orbiter (satellite photos from a later NASA mission in 2001 shattered the illusion of the original image).

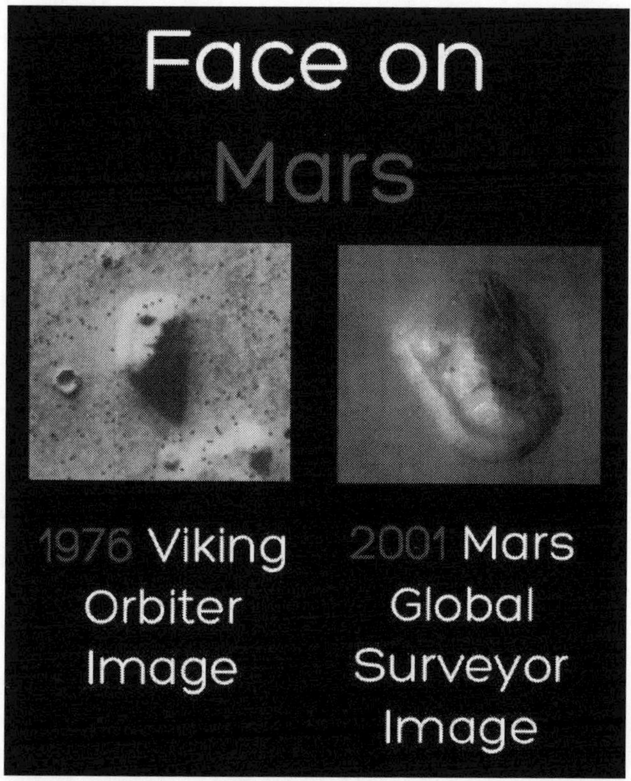

Another great example of pareidolia is the 'Virgin Mary' toast - a toasted cheese sandwich purportedly bearing the image of the Virgin Mary which sold on eBay for $28,000! You can get further details and see a picture of this very expensive lunch item via the following link.

http://news.bbc.co.uk/2/hi/4034787.stm

9. WILLIAM JAMES PSYCHOLOGY SUPERSTAR

If there was one person from psychology's past that I could invite to dinner it would be William James. James is rightly considered the founder of modern psychology, an accolade he shares with Wilhelm Wundt; however, in terms of promoting incredibly interesting psychology, William James wins hands down.

As Professor Richard Wiseman notes in his excellent book Rip it Up, "*Appalled by what he saw as the triviality of Wundt's work, James firmly believed that psychological research should be relevant to people's lives*". *He, therefore, set about investigating "far more interesting and pragmatic issues, including whether it was right to believe in God, what made life worth living, and if free will actually exists.*"

William James never missed an opportunity to study and report on something of human and psychological interest. For example, you would think that if you were caught up in the middle of a devastating natural disaster, the first thing on your mind would be to get as far away from danger as possible; however, this is the inimitable William James we're talking about!

When "The Great" San Francisco earthquake hit on the morning of April 18th, 1906, James was just 35 miles away at Stanford University. Close enough to have experienced the earthquake directly he was very keen to discover how his subjective experience of the event compared with those around him. And not just from the relatively safe confines of Stanford. On the day of the earthquake James made his way to San Francisco itself, which in his own words gave him and his "*valiant feminine escort some four hours of observation.*"

Here are William James's documented observations from that infamous day in history.

When I departed from Harvard for Stanford University last December, almost the last good-by I got was that of my old Californian friend B: "I hope they'll give you a touch of earthquake while you're there, so that you may also become acquainted with that Californian institution."

Accordingly, when, lying awake at about half past five on the morning of April 18 in my little "flat" on the campus of Stanford, I felt the bed begin to waggle, my first consciousness was one of gleeful recognition of the nature of the movement. "By Jove," I said to myself, "here's B's old earthquake, after all!" And then, as it went crescendo . "And a jolly good one it is, too!" I said.

Sitting up involuntarily, and taking a kneeling position, I was thrown down on my face as it went fortior shaking the room exactly as a terrier shakes a rat. Then everything that was on anything else slid off to the floor, over went bureau and chiffonier with a crash, as the fortissimo was reached; plaster cracked, an awful roaring noise seemed to fill the outer air, and in an instant all was still again, save the soft babble of human voices from far and near that soon began to make itself heard, as the inhabitants in costumes negligés in various degrees sought the greater safety of the street and yielded to the passionate desire for sympathetic communication.

The thing was over, as I understand the Lick Observatory to have declared, in forty-eight seconds. To me it felt as if about that length of time, although I have heard others say that it seemed to them longer. In my case, sensation and emotion were so strong that little thought, and no reflection or volition, were possible in the short time consumed by the phenomenon.

The emotion consisted wholly of glee and admiration; glee at the vividness which such an abstract idea or verbal term as "earthquake" could put on when translated into sensible reality and verified concretely; and admiration at the way in which the frail little wooden house could hold itself together in spite of such a shaking. I felt no trace whatever of fear; it was pure delight and welcome.

"Go it," I almost cried aloud, "and go it stronger!"

I ran into my wife's room, and found that she, although awakened from sound sleep, had felt no fear, either. Of all the persons whom I later interrogated, very few had felt any fear while the shaking lasted, although many had had a "turn," as they realized their narrow escapes from bookcases or bricks from chimney-breasts falling on their beds and pillows an instant after they had left them.

As soon as I could think, I discerned retrospectively certain peculiar ways in which my consciousness had taken in the phenomenon. These ways were quite spontaneous, and, so to speak, inevitable and irresistible.

First, I personified the earthquake as a permanent individual entity. It was the earthquake of my friend B's augury, which had been lying low and holding itself back during all the intervening months, in order, on that lustrous April morning, to invade my room, and energize the more intensely and triumphantly. It came, moreover, directly to me . It stole in behind my back, and once inside the room, had me all to itself, and could manifest itself convincingly. Animus and intent were never more present in any human action, nor did any human activity ever more definitely point back to a living agent as its source and origin.

All whom I consulted on the point agreed as to this feature in their experience. "It expressed intention," "It was vicious," "It was bent on destruction," "It wanted to show its power," or what not. To me, it wanted simply to manifest the full meaning of its name. But what was this "It"? To some, apparently, a vague demonic power; to me an individualized being, B's earthquake, namely.

One informant interpreted it as the end of the world and the beginning of the final judgment. This was a lady in a San Francisco hotel, who did not think of its being an earthquake till after she had got into the street and someone had explained it to her. She told me that the theological interpretation had kept fear from her mind, and made her take the shaking calmly. For "science," when the tensions in the earth's crust reach the breaking-point, and strata fall into an altered equilibrium, earthquake is simply the collective name of all the cracks and shakings and disturbances that happen. They are the earthquake. But for me the earthquake was the cause of the disturbances, and the perception of it as a living agent was irresistible. It had an overpowering dramatic convincingness.

I realize now better than ever how inevitable were men's earlier mythologic versions of such catastrophes, and how artificial and against the grain of our spontaneous perceiving are the later habits into which science educates us. It was simply impossible for untutored men to take earthquakes into their minds as anything but supernatural warnings or retributions.

A good instance of the way in which the tremendousness of a catastrophe may banish fear was given me by a Stanford student. He was in the fourth story of Encina Hall, an immense stone dormitory building. Awakened from sleep, he recognized what the disturbance was, and sprang from the bed, but was thrown off his feet in a moment, while his books and furniture fell round him. Then with an awful, sinister, grinding roar, everything gave way, and with chimneys, floor-beams, walls and all, he descended through the three lower stories of the building into the basement. "This is my end, this is my death," he felt; but all the while no trace of fear. The experience was too overwhelming for anything but passive surrender to it. (Certain heavy chimneys had fallen in, carrying the whole centre of the building with them.)

Arrived at the bottom, he found himself with rafters and débris round him, but not pinned in or crushed. He saw daylight, and crept toward it through the obstacles. Then, realizing that he was in his nightgown, and feeling no pain anywhere, his first thought was to get back to his room and find some more presentable clothing. The stairways at Encina Hall are at the ends of the building. He made his way to one of them, and went up the four flights, only to find his room no longer extant. Then he noticed pain in his feet, which had been injured, and came down the stairs with difficulty. When he talked with me ten days later he had been in hospital a week, was very thin and pale, and went on crutches, and was dressed in borrowed clothing.

So much for Stanford, where all our experiences seem to have been very similar. Nearly all our chimneys went down, some of them disintegrating from top to bottom; parlor floors were covered with bricks; plaster strewed the floors; furniture was everywhere upset and dislocated; but the wooden dwellings sprang back to their original position, and in house after house not a window stuck or a door scraped at top or bottom. Wood architecture was triumphant! Everybody was excited, but the excitement at first, at any rate, seemed to be almost joyous. Here at last was a real earthquake after so many years of harmless waggle! Above all, there was an irresistible desire to talk about it, and exchange experiences.

Most people slept outdoors for several subsequent nights, partly to be safer in case of recurrence, but also to work off their emotion, and get the full unusualness out of the experience. The vocal babble of early-waking girls and boys from the gardens of the campus, mingling with the birds' songs and the exquisite weather, was for three or four days delightful sunrise phenomenon.

Now turn to San Francisco, thirty-five miles distant, from which an automobile ere long brought us the dire news of a city in ruins, with fires beginning at various points, and the water-supply interrupted. I was fortunate enough to board the only train of cars — a very small one — that got up to the city; fortunate enough also to escape in the evening by the only train that left it. This gave me and my valiant feminine escort some four hours of observation. My business is with "subjective" phenomena exclusively; so I will say nothing of the material ruin that greeted us on every hand — the daily papers and the weekly journals have done full justice to that topic. By midday, when we reached the city, the pall of smoke was vast and the dynamite detonations had begun, but the troops, the police and the firemen seemed to have established order, dangerous neighborhoods were roped off everywhere and picketed, saloons closed, vehicles impressed, and every one at work who could work.

It was indeed a strange sight to see an entire population in the streets, busy as ants in an uncovered ant-hill scurrying to save their eggs and larvae. Every horse, and everything on wheels in the city, from hucksters' wagons to automobiles, was being loaded with what effects could be scraped together from houses which the advancing flames were threatening. The sidewalks were covered with well-dressed men and women, carrying baskets, bundles, valises, or dragging trunks to spots of greater temporary safety, soon to be dragged farther, as the fire kept spreading!

In the safer quarters, every doorstep was covered with the dwelling's tenants, sitting surrounded with their more indispensable chattels, and ready to flee at a minute's notice. I think everyone must have fasted on that day, for I saw no one eating. There was no appearance of general dismay, and little of chatter or of in-coordinated excitement.

Everyone seemed doggedly bent on achieving the job which he had set himself to perform; and the faces, although somewhat tense and set and grave, were inexpressive of emotion. I noticed only three persons overcome, two Italian women, very poor, embracing an aged fellow countrywoman, and all weeping. Physical fatigue and seriousness were the only inner states that one could read on countenances.

With lights forbidden in the houses, and the streets lighted only by the conflagration, it was apprehended that the criminals of San Francisco would hold high carnival on the ensuing night. But whether they feared the disciplinary methods of the United States troops, who were visible everywhere, or whether they were themselves solemnized by the immensity of the disaster, they lay low and did not "manifest," either then or subsequently.

The only very discreditable thing to human nature that occurred was later, when hundreds of lazy "bummers" found that they could keep camping in the parks, and make alimentary storage-batteries of their stomachs, even in some cases getting enough of the free rations in their huts or tents to last them well into the summer. This charm of pauperized vagabondage seems all along to have been Satan's most serious bait to human nature. There was theft from the outset, but confined, I believe, to petty pilfering.

Cash in hand was the only money, and millionaires and their families were no better off in this respect than any one. Whoever got a vehicle could have the use of it; but the richest often went without, and spent the first two nights on rugs on the bare ground, with nothing but what their own arms had rescued. Fortunately, those nights were dry and comparatively warm, and Californians are accustomed to camping conditions in the summer, so suffering from exposure was less great than it would have been elsewhere. By the fourth night, which was rainy, tents and huts had brought most campers under cover.

I went through the city again eight days later. The fire was out, and about a quarter of the area stood unconsumed. Intact skyscrapers dominated the smoking level majestically and superbly — they and a few walls that had survived the overthrow. Thus has the courage of our architects and builders received triumphant vindication!

The inert elements of the population had mostly got away, and those that remained seemed what Mr. H. G. Wells calls "efficients." Sheds were already going up as temporary starting-points of business. Everyone looked cheerful, in spite of the awful discontinuity of past and future, with every familiar association with material things dissevered; and the discipline and order were practically perfect.

As these notes of mine must be short, I had better turn to my more generalized reflections.

Two things in retrospect strike me especially, and are the most emphatic of all my impressions. Both are reassuring as to human nature.

The first of these was the rapidity of the improvisation of order out of chaos. It is clear that just as in every thousand human beings there will be statistically so many artists, so many athletes, so many thinkers, and so many potentially good soldiers, so there will be so many potential organizers in times of emergency. In point of fact, not only in the great city, but in the outlying towns, these natural ordermakers, whether amateurs or officials, came to the front immediately. There seemed to be no possibility which there was not someone there to think of, or which within twenty-four hours was not in some way provided for.

A good illustration is this: Mr. Keith is the great landscape-painter of the Pacific slope, and his pictures, which are many, are artistically and pecuniarily precious. Two citizens, lovers of his work, early in the day diverted their attention from all other interests, their own private ones included, and made it their duty to visit every place which they knew to contain a Keith painting. They cut them from their frames, rolled them up, and in this way got all the more important ones into a place of safety.

When they then sought Mr. Keith, to convey the joyous news to him, they found him still in his studio, which was remote from the fire, beginning a new painting. Having given up his previous work for lost, he had resolved to lose no time in making what amends he could for the disaster. The completeness of organization at Palo Alto, a town of ten thousand inhabitants close to Stanford University, was almost comical. People feared exodus on a large scale of the rowdy elements of San Francisco. In point of tact, very few refugees came to Palo Alto. But within twenty-four hours, rations, clothing, hospital, quarantine, disinfection, washing, police, military, quarters in camp and in houses, printed information, employment, all were provided for under the care of so many volunteer committees.

Much of this readiness was American, much of it Californian; but I believe that every country in a similar crisis would have displayed it in a way to astonish the spectators. Like soldiering, it lies always latent in human nature.

The second thing that struck me was the universal equanimity. We soon got letters from the East, ringing with anxiety and pathos; but I now know fully what I have always believed, that the pathetic way of feeling great disasters belongs rather to the point of view of people at a distance than to the immediate victims. I heard not a single really pathetic or sentimental word in California expressed by any one.

The terms "awful," "dreadful" fell often enough from people's lips, but always with a sort of abstract meaning, and with a face that seemed to admire the vastness of the catastrophe as much as it bewailed its cuttingness. When talk was not directly practical, I might almost say that it expressed (at any rate in the nine days I was there) a tendency more toward nervous excitement than toward grief. The hearts concealed private bitterness enough, no doubt, but the tongues disdained to dwell on the misfortunes of self, when almost everybody one spoke to had suffered equally.

Surely the cutting edge of all our usual misfortunes comes from their character of loneliness. We lose our health, our wife or children die, our house burns down, or our money is made way with, and the world goes on rejoicing, leaving us on one side and counting us out from all its business. In California every one, to some degree, was suffering, and one's private miseries were merged in the vast general sum of privation and in the all-absorbing practical problem of general recuperation. The cheerfulness, or, at any rate, the steadfastness of tone, was universal. Not a single whine or plaintive word did I hear from the hundred losers whom I spoke to. Instead of that there was a temper of helpfulness beyond the counting.

It is easy to glorify this as something characteristically American, or especially Californian. Californian education has, of course, made the thought of all possible recuperations easy. In an exhausted country, with no marginal resources, the outlook on the future would be much darker. But I like to think that what I write of is a normal and universal trait of human nature. In our drawing-rooms and offices we wonder how people ever do go through battles, sieges and shipwrecks. We quiver and sicken in imagination, and think those heroes superhuman. Physical pain whether suffered alone or in company, is always more or less unnerving and intolerable. But mental pathos and anguish, I fancy, are usually effects of distance. At the place of action, where all are concerned together, healthy animal insensibility and heartiness take their place. At San Francisco the need will continue to be awful, and there will doubtless be a crop of nervous wrecks before the weeks and months are over, but meanwhile the commonest men, simply because they are men, will go on, singly and collectively, showing this admirable fortitude of temper.

Principles of Psychology

It would be remiss of me to include a section on William James without mention of his scientific and literary masterpiece Principles of Psychology published in 1890. Widely cited as the most important text in the history of psychology, the following description of Principles of Psychology was published as part of a tribute to William James shortly after his death in 1910.

"*It is truly a remarkable book, combining physiology, pathological psychology, comparative psychology, experimental psychology, introspective psychology and philosophy into one whole which has dominated the science. The author is always accurate in his scientific material and clear in his statements, but frank in his criticism and daring in his conclusions. His own contributions on the stream of thought, the perception of things and of space, the emotions, instinct, habit and in many other directions are of fundamental importance. The work has an extraordinary vitality and individuality which make it a work of art and a classic.*"

I heartily recommend taking a look at Principles of Psychology and thanks to Christopher D. Green, professor of psychology and philosophy at York University in Toronto, Canada; you can read William James' seminal work for free via the following link.

psychclassics.yorku.ca/James/Principles

10. PSYCHOLOGY QUOTES

Did you know that there is no evidence to suggest that Sigmund Freud actually said "*Sometimes a cigar is just a cigar.*" You shouldn't be too surprised though because as Abraham Lincoln pointed out "*The problem with quotes on the Internet is that it is hard to verify their authenticity*!"

Here's a selection of the most liked, shared and commented upon quotes posted on the All About Psychology facebook page.

Everything that irritates us about others can lead to an understanding of ourselves. (Carl Jung)

Any theory that regards personality as stable, fixed or invariable is wrong. (Gordon Allport)

A musician must make music, an artist must paint, a poet must write, if he is to be ultimately happy. What a man can be, he must be. This need we may call self-actualization. (Abraham Maslow)

Self-belief does not necessarily ensure success, but self-disbelief assuredly spawns failure. (Albert Bandura).

We are what we are because we have been what we have been, and what is needed for solving the problems of human life and motives is not moral estimates but more knowledge. (Sigmund Freud).

Memory is not just the imprint of the past time upon us; it is the keeper of what is meaningful for our deepest hopes and fears. (Rollo May)

Color is powerful. It is almost physiologically impossible to be in a bad mood when you're wearing bright red pants. (Jessi Arrington)

Forgive me, for those of you who play the lottery but economists, at least among themselves, refer to the lottery as a stupidity tax, because the odds of getting any payoff by investing your money in a lottery ticket are approximately equivalent to flushing the money directly down the toilet. (Dan Gilbert)

The most powerful force ever known on this planet is human cooperation - a force for construction and destruction. (Jonathan Haidt)

If you want truly to understand something, try to change it. (Kurt Lewin)

A failure is not always a mistake; it may simply be the best one can do under the circumstances. The real mistake is to stop trying. (B.F. Skinner)

Hope is both the earliest and the most indispensable virtue inherent in the state of being alive. (Erik Erikson)

Psychology should be just as concerned with building strength as with repairing damage. (Martin Seligman)

The full illustrated psychology quotes collection can be found via the following link.

pinterest.com/psychology/psychology-quotes

11. FIFTY SHADES OF GREY (MINUS 49!)

Forget fifty shades of grey; it's time to spank your mind with just one!

The squares marked A and B are the same shade of grey!

This incredible illusion was created by Edward H. Adelson, Professor of Vision Science in the department of Brain and Cognitive Sciences at the Massachusetts Institute of Technology. According to Professor Adelson, the illusion is a product of your visual system attempting "*to determine where the shadows are and how to compensate for them, in order to determine the shade of grey "paint" that belongs to the surface.*"

Square B sits in the shadow of the cylinder, Square A does not and your perceptual field has evolved to automatically correct changes in the appearance of a color when it is in shadow. A great explanation as to why squares A and B appear so visually different has been offered by Richard Wiseman, Professor of the Public Understanding of Psychology at the University of Hertfordshire.

"*Your eyes and brain see that the two squares are the same shade of grey, but then think, 'Hold on - if a square in a shadow reflects the same amount of light as a square outside of the shadow, then in reality it must be a much lighter shade of grey.' As a result, your brain alters your perception of the image so that you see what it thinks is out there in the real world.*"

If you still don't believe that the squares marked A and B are the same shade of gray, this should help convince you.

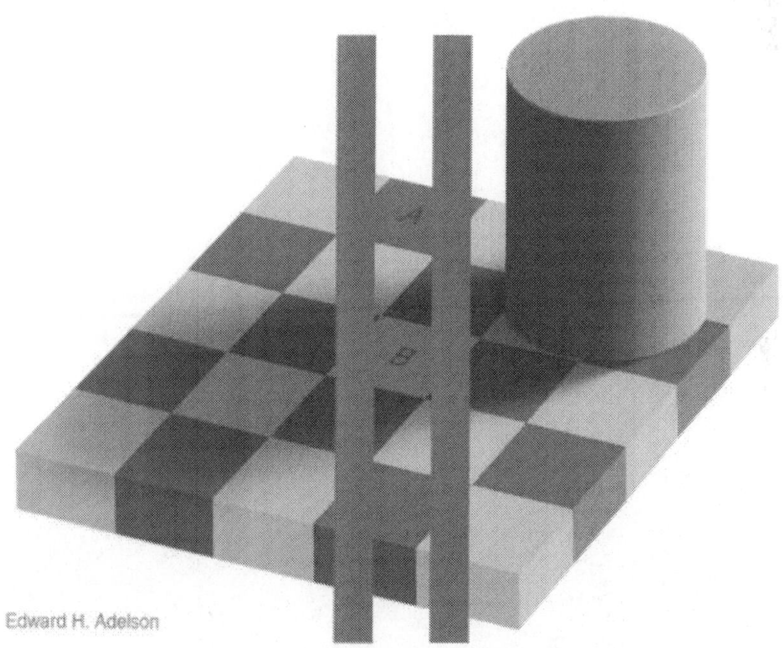

By joining the squares marked A and B with two vertical stripes of the same shade of grey, it becomes apparent that both squares are the same.

If you would like even more proof make sure you check out Professor Adelson's more evidence web page

persci.mit.edu/gallery/checkershadow/more_evidence

An Enduring Topic of Interest

Optical illusions have long been a source of psychological interest, particularly in relation to visual perception, sensory processes and attention. The following extract from 1897 for example is taken from an article written by E.W Scripture from Yale University entitled "Sources of The New Psychology."

"*The physiology of the eye originated much of the psychology of sight. Concerning the functions of the optical system, physiology can scarcely be said to have gone beyond the dioptrics of the eye. Nearly all further knowledge consists of deductions from the mental experiences of the subject. For example, physiology knows almost nothing concerning the functions of the retina. Psychologically, however, the color sensations and their combinations can be accurately measured.*

It is true that the investigations of color vision have been and are mainly carried out by physiologists and physicists; but the point of view has become primarily a purely psychological one. This is strikingly exemplified in the researches of Konig, from which physiological deductions are practically excluded. For the various other phenomena, such as those of the optical illusions, of monocular and of binocular space, we have at present no hope of anything beyond a psychological knowledge, and the investigations of Hering, Helmholtz, and others can be regarded as direct contributions to psychology."

Learn More

Michael Bach a vision scientist from the University of Freiburg has put together a wonderful collection of visual phenomena and optical Illusions. See following link.

michaelbach.de/ot/index.html

Remember sometimes seeing is deceiving

12. I DON'T THINK, THEREFORE, I AM

"When I step onto the court, I don't have to think about anything."

(Michael Jordan)

Just like basketball legend Michael Jordan there are lots of things you do automatically without having to think about it. Walking, riding a bike, typing your PIN number into an ATM, tying your shoelaces etc.

Our ability to operate on autopilot is typically a result of having repeated a task so many times that it no longer requires any conscious effort on our part for it to be successfully carried out.

Remember when you first started learning to drive? All that focused attention! Wondering how you would ever master having to do several things at once. Now look at you! Chances are you will have driven somewhere recently and got to your destination with little or no memory of the trip?

The notion that there are two very different levels of mental processing - level one involving willful rational thought and a spontaneous, automatic, unthinking level two - has been a topic of abiding interest within psychology.

In the founding days of the discipline it was interest in level one which held sway. When Wilhelm Wundt established the first experimental psychology laboratory in 1879, he championed the use of introspection (the examination of conscious thoughts, feelings and experience) as the primary basis of psychological research.

At the start of the 20th Century there was then a sustained period within psychology where interest in level two predominated. Most notably as a result of Sigmund Freud's influential work on "*The Unconscious*," where primal inner drives and forces residing outside our awareness were said to be directing and influencing our behavior. However, this concept along with other core ideas within Freudian psychoanalysis were largely discredited within academic psychology on the grounds of being too vague and untestable.

There was then a dormant period of investigation until the start of the 1980's when cognitive psychologists began to develop innovative methods for studying unconscious processes. Among the most influential movements within this new psychological paradigm, was social cognition; an approach to studying designed to explore the mental mechanisms by which information within a social context is processed and applied.

Social cognition has been examined in relation to a wide range of social interactions, for example, how we form impressions of the people we meet. It has also been employed to help make sense of the social attitudes (both positive and negative) people hold when thinking about gender, age, race and sexual orientation etc.

Take a moment to consider your own attitudes on the following topics. Gun control, global warming, the death penalty, drug legalization, euthanasia, health care, gay marriage.

You probably have strong views on one or more of these topics, but how did the attitudes you hold come about? I highlighted above the notion that there are two very different levels of mental processing - level one involving willful rational thought and a spontaneous, automatic, unthinking level two. I imagine as far as your attitudes are concerned you would argue that level one mental processing came into play i.e., your attitudes formed as a result of conscious rational thought on your part.

You Know Your Own Mind, Right?

Well, maybe not as much as you quite literally would like to think, because according to pioneers within the field of Implicit Social Cognition (research concerning thoughts and feelings that occur outside of conscious awareness or control.) "*The truth is that thoughts, feelings, and behavior operate largely without deliberation or conscious recognition.*" (Mahzarin Banaji)

Not convinced? Why not put this idea to the test.

Project Implicit

Founded in 1998 by Anthony Greenwald (University of Washington), Mahzarin Banaji (Harvard University), and Brian Nosek (University of Virginia), Project Implicit was established as a "virtual laboratory" where members of the public have the opportunity "*to assess their conscious and unconscious preferences for over 90 different topics ranging from pets to political issues, ethnic groups to sports teams, and entertainers to styles of music.*" See following link for full details.

implicit.harvard.edu/implicit/research

I highly recommend taking a test or two. It might not change the way you think but it might just change the way you think about how you think you think!

If you would like to learn more about this fascinating topic I highly recommend reading "Blindspot: Hidden Biases of Good People by Mahzarin Banaji and Anthony Greenwald.

"Your assumptions are your windows on the world. Scrub them off every once in a while, or the light won't come in."

(Isaac Asimov)

13. PSYCHOLOGY WORTH TALKING ABOUT

If I had to pick a favorite website it would be TED.Com. The concept behind TED is just brilliant, namely bring together the world's most fascinating thinkers and doers, and challenge them to give the talk of their lives in 18 minutes. The following extract from the website says it all really.

"*We believe passionately in the power of ideas to change attitudes, lives and ultimately, the world. So we're building here a clearinghouse that offers free knowledge and inspiration from the world's most inspired thinkers, and also a community of curious souls to engage with ideas and each other.*"

Included among the most fascinating, engaging and thought provoking psychology related talks are:

The Psychology of Evil

Philip Zimbardo knows how easy it is for nice people to turn bad. In this talk, he shares insights and graphic unseen photos from the Abu Ghraib trials. Then he talks about the flip side: how easy it is to be a hero, and how we can rise to the challenge.

What Our Language Habits Reveal

Steven Pinker looks at language and how it expresses what goes on in our minds and how the words we choose communicate much more than we realize.

The Brain in Love

Why do we crave love so much, even to the point that we would die for it? To learn more about our very real, very physical need for romantic love, Helen Fisher and her research team took MRIs of people in love and people who had just been dumped.

The Mystery of Chronic Pain

We think of pain as a symptom, but there are cases where the nervous system develops feedback loops and pain becomes a terrifying disease in itself. Starting with the story of a girl whose sprained wrist turned into a nightmare, Elliot Krane talks about the complex mystery of chronic pain, and reviews the facts we're just learning about how it works and how to treat it.

What Do Babies Think?

Alison Gopnik takes us into the fascinating minds of babies and children, and shows us how much we understand before we even realize we do.

How To Spot A Liar

On any given day we're lied to from 10 to 200 times, and the clues to detect those lie can be subtle and counter-intuitive. Pamela Meyer shows the manners and "hotspots" used by those trained to recognize deception.

You can watch all of the excellent psychology related talks featured above, along with many others via a video playlist I have created as part of my All About Psychology YouTube channel. See following link.

www.youtube.com/playlist?list=PLFDE868BCF58A3950

14. PUT YOURSELF TO THE TEST

Here are three quick tests that you will really enjoy doing, and I bet you will get your family and friends to have a go as well! Please note that you will need a reliable and preferably high-speed online Internet connection. To do each test, simply visit the appropriate link below.

TEST 1: POWERS OF PERCEPTION

See following link to watch a video created by the Open University designed to test your powers of perception.

www.all-about-psychology.com/powers-of-perception.html

TEST 2: CAN YOU SPOT A FAKE SMILE?

Based on research by Professor Paul Ekman this online experiment is designed to test whether you can spot the difference between a fake smile and a real one. See following link to test how accurate you are in emotional recognition.

www.bbc.co.uk/science/humanbody/mind/surveys/smiles/index.shtml

TEST 3: HOW WELL DO YOU READ OTHER PEOPLE?

In this short quiz produced by the greater good science center at the University of California, Berkeley, you will be asked to identify the emotion conveyed in 20 facial expression photos. The quiz is designed to measure your emotional intelligence and draws on pioneering research by psychologists Paul Ekman and Dacher Keltner. See following link to test how well you read other people.

greatergood.berkeley.edu/ei_quiz

15. OLD SCHOOL PSYCHOLOGY

Showcasing genuine reports, images and research findings from the past.

By the Power of Grayskull! Marriage Makes A Man's mind More Feminine (1929)

Marriage makes a man's mind more feminine, Prof. L.M. Terman, of Stanford University, declared in a paper he submitted to the congress. Having analyzed masculine and feminine traits in the minds of large groups of men and women, he reported that environment often plays an overwhelming part in shaping them.

A "he-man" in appearance may be more feminine in thought than the average woman, he said, since physical appearance has nothing to do with the mind in either sex. After a few years of marriage husbands, he found, are likely to take on a more feminine outlook in interests, preferences and emotional reactions.

As someone who grew up in the 1980's I couldn't resist picking up on the He-Man reference!

Easily Excited Brunettes (1932)

Prof. W. M. Marston, of Columbia University, made scientific tests with a blonde and a brunette to determine emotional reactions. Results indicated brunettes are higher keyed

Useless Things Psychologists Have Taught us! (1923)

The popular idea that it "takes a big man to be a salesman" was exploded recently by a scientific study of the sales records of 600 salesmen, which proved that the most successful selling is done by men of about five feet nine inches tall.

Dr. Harry D. Kitson, of Indiana University, recently presented the findings of this research to the American Psychological Association.

Puma Calls For Food By Firing A Cannon (1935)

Training by laboratory workers has overcome the puma's fear of firearms

Though most animals are gun-shy, a wild puma kept at a laboratory in Moscow, Russia, deliberately fires a cannon to signify that it is hungry. Laboratory workers trained the animal, in accordance with the theories of Dr. Ivan Pavlov, noted physiologist, by firing the piece and giving the puma a piece of meat after each shot. Soon it overcame its natural dislike for the sound and learned to get its meals by climbing upon a platform and pulling the firing cord.

Psychopathic Laboratory (1916)

The following magazine picture was used to help publicize the opening of the New York Police Department Psychopathic Laboratory. As an interesting side note, Edward Thorndike "*Father of modern educational psychology*" was on the Psychopathic Laboratory advisory board.

Inspector Faurot turning over a case to the psychologist at the psychopathic laboratory at police headquarters. The inspector, at the right, is handing the history of the case to the psychologist

A physician making an examination of a prisoner at the psychopathic laboratory

Pavlov's Dog (1909)

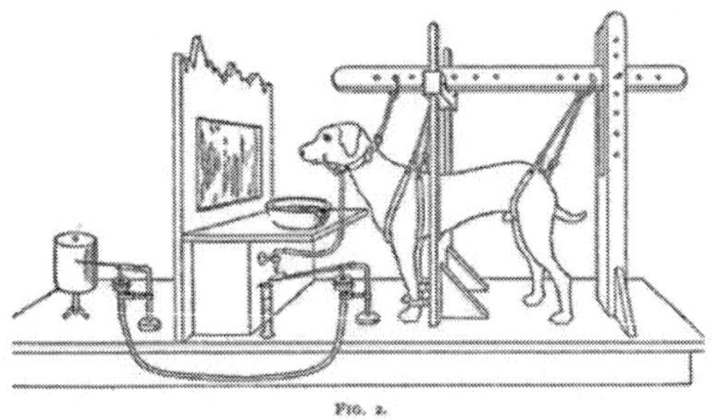

Original illustration from an article entitled *The Method of Pavlov in Animal Psychology.* The text accompanying the illustration was as follows: *A dog whose normal salivary reaction had been carefully observed and in which the habit of responding to a certain sound had been developed was placed in apparatus similar to that of Fig. 2.*

Moral and Physical Causes of Insanity (1860)

Moral Causes.		Physical Causes.		
Domestic troubles and griefs	928	Ill-health and unclassified diseases	2388	3067
Religious anxiety	792	Fevers	199	
Mental anxiety	721	Epilepsy	319	
Financial difficulties, reverses of fortune, &c.	652	Cerebral disease	117	
Loss of friends	585	Paralysis	44	
Disappointment in love, ambition, &c.	576	Intemperance and dissipation		1202
Excessive study or application to business	165	Conditions peculiar to women		891
Fear and fright	126	Vicious habits and indulgences		514
Defective education	37	Wounds and blows		250
Uncontrollable temper	32	Excessive use of opium, tobacco, &c.		129
Nostalgia	29	Exposure and loss of sleep		123
Political excitement	22	Spiritualism		94
Unclassified moral causes	40	Exposure to sun or heat		74
		Over-exertion		62
		Old age		32
		Unclassified physical causes		172
Total	4649	Total		6610

Historical gem from the days when attitudes and knowledge towards mental illness were different to say the least. I love the idea of "*political excitement*" being a moral cause of insanity and I would love to know what the "*conditions peculiar to women*" which accounted for 891 physical causes of insanity!

The Szondi Test (1948)

Great picture of the Szondi Test in action in which the subject is asked to decide which faces he likes and which he dislikes. This classic projective test of personality is named after the Hungarian psychiatrist Léopold Szondi and is based on his theory of genotropism (reciprocal attraction) which suggests that photo choice is reflective of the test takers own pathology.

The photographs shown to the subject are of persons diagnosed with disorders such as manic-depressive psychosis, paranoia, schizophrenia, hysteria and sadism.

Pigeon Ping Pong (1950)

Wonderful picture relating to B.F Skinner's research into the theory that reward is more effective in getting people - or in this case pigeons - to perform tasks. The text accompanying the photo was as follows: *In still another of Professor Skinner's exhibits, which demonstrates competition, the birds play a modified game of ping-pong. Considerably smaller than regulation size, being about two feet square, and has no net. One pigeon, using his beak, tries to bat the ball past his opponent. Rallies sometimes go to three or four shots but most of the shots are "aces." The winner is rewarded with food after each shot.*

School Psychology (1908)

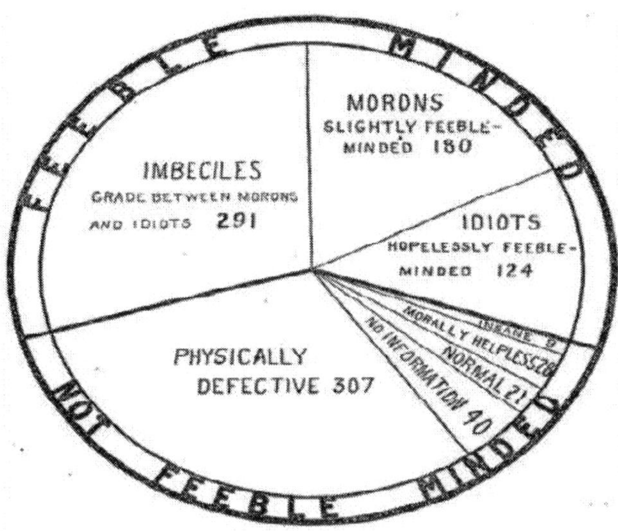

Pie chart from an article entitled "Nearly 15,000 School Children Are Defectives.

Social Stimulus (1929)

Speaking at the International Congress of Psychology at Yale University in 1929 Professor Mark A. May noted that the effect upon others of an individual's physique, dress code, quality of voice and choice of language may be rolled into one to produce a Social Stimulus Value rating from 0 to 100%.

For instance, a person who can enter a room without attracting the slightest recognition of his or her presence from others, by word to glance rates "zero" on the Social Stimulus personality test.

I bet you will be rating people this weekend!

16. YOU MAY BE A LITTLE SMUG. AND YOU LIKE GRAVY

Believe it or not, the title above is taken from a personality profile compiled by "color experts" in relation to people who prefer the color brown!

Brown was just one of the colors featured in an old article from 1940 which claimed that color engineers had discovered a close connection between a person's color preferences and their personality.

When I shared these brilliantly ridiculous color psychology profiles on facebook etc, I made it very clear that it was just for fun and not to be taken seriously. Apart from anything else it would seem that only men have personalities worth exploring in this way.

Anyway, over to the "color experts."

YELLOW

If you like yellow, you are probably the intellectual type, with a philosophy of your own and a hankering to reform others and convert them to your way of thinking. You have a keen mind but are handicapped by intolerance and lack of human sympathy.

PURPLE

Purple is the color of royalty and although royalty is out of date, purple is still affected by persons with a tendency to be vain, selfish, and egotistical. They like to think themselves superior to others, through the opinion is not always shared by their friends. However, a taste for purple may be accompanied by the more desirable royal quality of magnanimity.

ORANGE

If you like orange, you are what people call a "good fellow" - a lover of companionship and conviviality. Wine, women and song are your dish. You like to talk and are good at it, though you are not sure to hold the same opinion for two days in a row. Unfortunately, your friendships are neither deep nor lasting. Likable personality and quick wit make you a good salesman.

BLUE

Blue is the color of the conservative, self-controlled character. If you lean to this hue in your clothing and surroundings, you are likely to have sound judgment and a strong sense of duty. On the other hand, you may have a tendency to take yourself and your affairs a little too seriously. You could have a better time if you could only learn to let yourself go.

RED

Is red your favorite color? Then you are probably impulsive, with strong desires and a liking for action and excitement. You may manage to conceal your emotions, but they are there just the same. Fickleness and a lack of perseverance are your greatest handicaps. Learn to manage and direct your strong passions and they will give you the rich life that you crave.

GREEN

People who prefer green are the happy average folks - good friends, good neighbors, good mixers. They like to belong to clubs and societies, read new books, see the new movies and plays. They know the value of money, but they're willing to part with it for a good cause. Their liking for the "good things of life" - wealth, comfort, social position - is sincere.

BROWN

Do you choose brown suits, brown shirts, brown ties? Then, the color experts say, you have substantial common sense. You prefer old fashioned things, and have no use for fads. Though your life is so well regulated that some may call you "set in your ways," you have little interest in the affairs of the rest of humanity. You may be a little smug. And you like gravy.

Amazingly, despite my insistence that this was just for fun and that the color profiles had no scientific credibility whatsoever, the following comments were posted in response.

75% correct!

Blue for me - self controlled? Yeah - but not conservative

Red is almost correct about me

Surprising its 70% correct!

Orange is me!

I think blue is my color

Strangely accurate

Yeah its 70% true but I still need to find myself in this color chart.

And my favorite comment...

Where the shitbrix is PINK?

The explanation as to why some people were seemingly convinced by the accuracy of the color based personality profiles can be found in chapter 1. I Can Read You Like A Book.

17. TO SLEEP, PERCHANCE TO DREAM

"It does not do to dwell on dreams and forget to live."

(Albus Dumbledore in J.K. Rowling's, Harry Potter and the Philosopher's Stone)

Dreams have been a source of unabated fascination since time immemorial. Consider for a moment the countless books, movies, poems, paintings and songs on the topic. The picture above by Robert William Buss for instance is widely considered the most famous image of Charles Dickens. Entitled Dickens' Dream it depicts the great author asleep in his chair dreaming about the wonderful characters he created. Sadly the picture remained unfinished as Buss died before its completion. You can see the full version of the Dickens' Dream painting via the following link.

commons.wikimedia.org/wiki/File:Dickens_dream.jpg

Psychology's contribution to our understanding of the meaning and purpose of dreams is a very important one. For example, dream expert Professor G. William Domhoff notes that although their ideas on the subject do not stand up to scientific scrutiny both Sigmund Freud and Carl Jung deserve credit for being "*the people who told us that dreams have psychological meaning as opposed to religious of prophetic meaning, which is what most people believed before they came along.* "

Spanning over fifty years, Professor Domhoff's own interest and research into dreams is as prolific as it is informative. His dream bank consists of over 20,000 dream reports drawn from a variety of reliable sources e.g., dream reports obtained from sleep laboratories, dream reports collected by anthropologists in small traditional societies and individual dream reports recorded in dream journals.

Armed with a remarkable amount of dream data and a method by which to make sense of it, namely, Content Analysis - *a technique allowing dream researchers to generate objective categories within which all the elements appearing frequently in dreams can be systematically assigned, counted and compared* - Professor Domhoff has been able to identify a series of consistent findings regarding the content of nightly dreams, for instance he found that:

Men dream more often of other men whereas women dream equally of men and women.

Dreams are much more likely to include negative elements, aggression, misfortunes, failures, negative emotions etc than positive emotions such as friendly interactions, good fortune, successes, happiness or joy.

Women dream more often of people they know, whereas in men's dreams there are more strangers.

Most dreams are about familiar topics which reflect our waking thoughts and concerns (this is known as the continuity hypothesis.)

The content of most dreams is not bizarre as people tend to think.

The "Purpose" of Dreams

As a result of his own dream research and having reviewed the evidence from scientific findings elsewhere, Professor Domhoff has come to embrace the cognitive perspective on dreams which suggests that dreams serve no adaptive function and are most likely "*the accidental byproduct of our ability to think complex thoughts and also our ability to create mental imagery in our waking life.*"

For a much more detailed account of Professor Domhoff's research findings I highly recommend watching a lecture he gave entitled *The Awesome Lawfulness of Your Nightly Dreams*. See following link.

www.youtube.com/watch?v=e6qhwdTzilg

Note To Psychology Students

Collecting dream reports and comparing them with waking thought reports from the same people would be an excellent topic to choose as part of a research project or final year thesis/dissertation. In the lecture mentioned above, Professor Domhoff highlights this as a potentially enlightening but as yet uncharted area of investigation Not only would research of this kind be able to test the hypothesis that dream content may not be as bizarre as we think, but it would also allow researchers to explore the converse possibility that waking thought is more bizarre than we care to admit.

If you are considering doing any research in relation the quantitative study of dreams *dreamresearch.net* is quite simply a must visit website. See following link.

www2.ucsc.edu/dreams

Classic Dream Articles

Just for fun, here are two dream articles from the past which I think you will enjoy reading.

Common Dreams (James J. Walsh 1925)

A travelling salesman recently consulted me after dreaming that he had fallen 15 stories from the roof of a high office building. He had awakened just before he struck the ground. The man frequently dreamed of falling, it seemed, and he had heard it said that if ever one hit bottom in a falling dream, the shock would mean instant death. Was it true?

Of course such an idea is ridiculous, but then, thousands of people believe that fairy tale. I should like to have reassured my patient with indisputable facts, but his question could be answered only with direct testimony. If any man has died from the shock of landing at the bottom of a dream precipice, he has not had the chance to tell us about it.

My traveling man's dream was easily explained. It was nature's alarm clock to let him know that his legs were getting an insufficient supply of blood. He had eaten a heavy meal just before retiring, and the weight was pressing on the big artery over the spine, interfering slightly with the blood going to the limbs. This produced the same sensation experienced in descending in a fast elevator. Gravity being interfered with, he was catching up with the blood being pumped into his legs. The result was a feeling of being without foundation.

I asked him, too, about the condition of his bedsprings, for probably more than half of all falling dreams are incited by the dreamer turning over and sliding into a depression in the bed. Further, I learned that about a week previously, my patient had been watching a daredevil perform hair-raising stunts on the edge of the roof of a high office building. He had been deeply impressed by the danger of these spectacular feats. Then when he experienced the falling sensation, the thoughts recently associated with it came readily in the form of a dream.

Many persons are afraid of their dreams. Superstition has more power in this field than in almost any other. It is because human knowledge of dreams has come so slowly. For thousands of years scientists have been attempting to pry beneath the darkened glass that has obscured this mysterious function of the human mind, and even yet, they sometimes have to answer, "I do not know."

In the last 20 years we have made much more progress in understanding dreams than in the centuries before. We are at last seeing possible answers to the recurring questions of mankind: "What are dreams? What causes them? What do they mean?"

Our most recent and significant experiments all point toward external causes for dreams. Thought processes, it is assumed, are going on all the time in our brains, at night, as well as during the day. The more complex functions, such as judgment and reasoning, ordinarily do not take place in sleep, allowing thinking to take the form of loose associations.

Recently science has taken dreams into the laboratory in an attempt to analyze them and determine their causes. Experiments with drugs show a definite relationship between external causes and dreams. They show definitely that dreams can be made to order.

One physician gave a woman patient a grain a day of extract of the pituitary gland to build up her blood pressure. After 10 days she began having very pleasant and satisfying dreams. Before, her dreams had been trivial, but now she began traveling to foreign lands, as she had always wanted to do. Everywhere she went, she saw beautiful landscapes in colors.

When the treatment was altered and adrenalin, another gland extract, was substituted, at once a change came over the nature of her dreams. They lost their colors and became terrifying, filled with violent quarrels. Chemists and physicians know that in normal anger or fear the human body secretes adrenalin from the suprarenal glands. This secretion makes our hair stand on end, a cold sweat appear, and the skin look like goose flesh. The experiment I have just mentioned showed that adrenalin treatments produced the same effect in the patient's dreams. An overdose of insulin, the newly discovered gland secretion, was found to produce the same feeling of fear.

Maurey, a noted French psychologist, first suggested that a physical cause was responsible for dreams. He told of one of his own dreams as an example. Just before going to bed he had been reading about the horrors of the French Revolution. When he fell asleep, he dreamed that he, too, was taken to the guillotine. His head was fitted on the block. Down came the gleaming, keen-edged knife, swiftly and more swiftly. Then, to his intense agony, it hit him and he woke in a cold sweat, to find that a light curtain rod had fallen and struck him squarely across the neck.

The falling rod did not just happen to hit him at the dramatic moment. The rod hit him first, he reasoned, and as the sensation penetrated his consciousness the events about which he had been reading recently flashed into his mind. Thus it is that most, if not all, of our dreams can be traced to an external physical cause coupled with an association of ideas born of our waking experience.

Examination of thousands of dreams experienced by thousands dreamers, has enabled us to learn that the most common dreams are eight in number. And every one of these can be traced to some physical cause.

The most common dream of all is said to be that of wandering about with insufficient clothing. In this, almost always the dreamer wakes to find that the bed-clothing has fallen from him, leaving some part of his body uncovered.

Most of us have dreamed of running after something, a trolley-car, for example. It is terrible, for in the dream your feet are fastened to the ground. Exerting every muscle and breathing as hard as you can, you make no progress. The car disappears in the distance. Then you wake, to find that your nose is stuffed up with cold and you are out of breath - again an actual physical sensation.

Another common dream is that of flying. Its cause is similar to that of falling. When you sleep, your diaphragm is less active and more breathing is done by the chest. Some slight interference with normal respiration causes consciousness of the chest moving up and down in quick, rhythmic movements. You have been lying in one position so long that the skin has become numb and no contact is felt with the bed. Feeling light and without contact with the earth, you dream of flying.

Since the invention of airplanes, dreams of flying have increased. Our dreams may use any material stored up in our brains. All of us have many images of airplanes and other aircraft at call. With dirigibles now soaring over our heads, dreamers will add rides in airships to their list of interesting experiences.

The dream of food, another common experience, usually can be traced to the sensation of hunger. I attach so much importance to this stimulus that when a man asks, "Why do I dream?" I often reply with the question, "When, or what did you eat?"

Ernest Shackleton, the British explorer, has told me about many of his dreams in the South Polar regions - most of them about food, all of them due to acute hunger. Once, with two companions, he was separated from the rest of his party. Each of the half starved men had three large crackers a day. They ate these slowly, reaching out after every crumb. One night, then, Shackleton dreamed that he was at the Lord Mayor's Banquet in London. All the viands for the entire meal were on the table at once, quite contrary to the usual custom. Shackleton was just ready to take the first mouthful, when he woke to find himself with a painfully empty stomach, on an iceberg in a frozen land.

An old Persian legend tells of a man called Barmecide who used to torture victims, kept three days without food or water, by setting before them empty dishes and asking them to partake of the appetizing delicacies that he described. Most of those who "feast with the Barmecide" in their dreams could avoid this unpleasant experience by drinking a glass of warm milk before retiring.

Dreams of murder and death usually are traceable to indigestion. A piece of cheese has been responsible for many a nightmare. In such a dream one feels something seriously wrong, and in tempting to find an explanation for it, memory brings out from the store house, the brain, the most terrifying images laid up there. So, too, any alteration of the blood supply to the teeth, or dental decay, may bring a dream that you are in the dentist's chair.

If, in early life, you have taken your school work seriously, you probably dream often of taking examinations. Men have told me that as much as 50 years after graduation, they have dreamed of examinations, and of being asked questions they cannot answer. This often is caused by anxiety over the next day's tasks. There is a sensation of unrest, and the dreamer, seeking some reason for it, associates it with an occasion when such uneasiness was felt - examination day at school. This type of dream is frequently experienced by doctors, lawyers, and other professional people who often are asked many questions.

The amazing ability of the memory to produce long forgotten thoughts and images was vividly demonstrated in an experience of a friend of Samuel Butler, English novelist. This occurred in his waking hours, but it has particular bearing on dreams.

The young man, 25 years old, tore the quick of his finger on a sliver. As he felt the pain, he remembered that he had had the same sensation at another time. It was when he was seven years old. He had poked his finger in a hole in the bed, in which a bolt had once fitted, and in doing this he had hurt his finger. He remembered that at the time he had picked up a piece of paper and had stuffed it in the hole.

Then his thoughts started on a different channel. About that time a five-pound note had been lost in the house and never found. Suddenly now, 18 years later, there came the thought, "Perhaps that bit of paper I stuffed into the hole was the missing money." The grown man was so curious that he boarded a train and went to the house in which he had lived as child. The bed was still there, but a bolt had been fitted into the hole. He removed the bolt, and there at the bottom of the hole was the missing note!

Thus was a long and complicated train of thought started by a sensation. In our dreams we sometimes find similar complexity. So many things happen, and they are so interesting, that we often remark upon awaking from a dream, "It was a regular play."

Often in such dreams, the dreamer finds himself taking the part of one of the leading characters. He is brilliant, much more clever than when awake, and talks with great wit. But it is significant that he never can remember this witty conversation after waking. He simply has a pleasurable sensation of having been important and clever. This is due to illusion. The same effect would be produced by a large quantity of champagne.

Books of dream poems have been written in which thoughts occurring in dreams are printed in black and white, but these were the result of somnambulism, which in often confused with dreaming.

Somnambulism, which is automatic activity of the brain, explains how men in their sleep sometimes work out problems which they were unable to work while awake. This automatic functioning, which is identical with reasoning done in the daytime, except that it is done in an unconscious state, is sometimes very dangerous. Working in the night as well as in the day, the brain gets no rest and is soon overtaxed.

The clarity of a dream depends altogether on the time it takes one to wake up. As thoughts gather around a sensation, they result in a curious conglomeration, which you straighten out after waking, unconsciously adding fitting elements to them. After a man tells a dream three of four times, it can hardly be recognized as the same narrative. Ordinarily, a dream lasts half a minute or so, although I have heard persons declare seriously that they have "dreamed for hours."

An old man told me recently of a dream of being chased. He was back in the valley in which he had lived as a child. He ran for hours, terrified and shrieking, yet his pursuers gained on him. At last he felt he was lost, and fell to the ground. His wife was shaking him. "Calvin," she said, "you have been asleep for two minutes, and you have been struggling like a madman for the last half minute."

Do dreams mean anything? Thousands of dream books have been written and no doubt interest in the subject will persist until the end of time, but if I had to answer the question with "yes" or "no," I should choose an emphatic "no." Since dreams are incited by physical causes they often tell of disturbances in the body. Some of these are obvious to the dreamer and some are not. A dream may reveal the presence of an illness of which the dreamer is unaware, since in sleep all of the senses are extremely acute. One of my patients, for example, had a series of dreams that a wildcat was clawing at his throat. I discovered that his was suffering from cancer of the throat.

But only in the disclosure of physical disorders or similar things, do dreams have meaning. I have no faith in what are commonly known as "prophetic dreams," those that tell one where to find lost finger-rings and missing wills.

I was talking recently with two sisters about dreams. One of them said "Oh, sister knows all about dreams. They were making a race book down at her office, and one of the horses was named 'Superbum.' Grace had a dream in which she saw bowls of soup. She went down the next morning and bet her money on Superbum, and, do you know she won, 15 to one?"

What could I say? Soup and Superbum! Surely an omen! All that I can say now is that that young woman is going lose hundreds of dollars in her lifetime if she keeps on placing her bets according to her dreams.

For every dream of prophecy that comes true, there are 999 that do not. Scarcely a ship sails out to sea without carrying on board at least one passenger who has dreamed that that particular ship will be wrecked during the voyage. What chance has one to prove dreams false prophets when such is the case?

"Facts" About Dreams (Lawrence Galton 1961)

All of us know we need sleep. But what we haven't known is that, even more than sleep, we need dreams. Without them, we'd go nuts. Not even scientists suspected that until a few months ago. While men of every age have speculated on the mystery of dreams, it's only recently that scientists have stopped speculating.

With completely new methods for looking into what goes on in our minds at night, they have been upsetting a great many old misconceptions and superstitions, discovering one fascinating fact after another, and building up a whole new science of dreams. Here's a look at what they've been finding out.

Research Shows That All of us Dream Every Night

And not just one dream, either. Each of us averages four to seven a night. We spend 1.5 hours or more - about 20 percent of our sleep time - in dreaming.

That's clear from years of research. It got started in 1952 because of accidental observation. While studying sleep cycles in infants, Prof. Nathaniel Kleitman and his associates at the University of Chicago

Sleep Laboratory noticed that tots' eyes kept moving under their lids after all other body movements had stopped.

To find out more, the Chicago investigators had adult volunteers sleep on cots in the laboratory and stuck tiny electrodes on their eye sockets so electric recordings could be made of eye movements. Night after night, every sleeper showed jerky eye activity. The jerky movements came in clusters several times a night. Still puzzled, the investigators stuck some more electrodes on the sleepers' scalps so brain waves could be recorded. And they found distinctive brain-wave patterns showing up whenever the jerk eye movements appeared.

Could the brain and eye activity indicate dreaming? It was only a hunch, but sure enough when sleepers were awakened immediately after a burst of rapid eye movements they reported they had been dreaming. When they were awakened at other times - no dreams.

Although investigators haven't been able to monitor the sleep of everybody in the country, the evidence that everybody dreams every night is strong. For in all sleepers studied, consistently recurring dream patterns have been found, even in those who said they never dream.

Why We Forget Many of our Dreams

We're ashamed of them - so we suppress them. That's been one theory. It may be true to some extent. But other factors have been uncovered.

Dreams tend to burst apart quickly. Drunks and drugged people are notorious for having trouble remembering. And dreams involve a low-grade type of mental activity, using brain mechanisms much like those used by the drunk and drugged. Lab work has shown that if you delay awakening a dreamer even just five minutes after the end of the eye movements, the chances of dream recall are greatly reduced.

After another five or ten minutes, there's very little chance at all of recall.

So ability to recall a dream may depend upon whether you happen to be dreaming at, or very shortly before, the time you wake up. There's a "tune-in" factor, too. Says Dr. Joe Kamiya of the University of Chicago: "I have observed prospective subjects who told me they very rarely dreamed but who began remembering dreams at home the day following my interview with them. So it seems to be a matter of attention - whether we are 'tuned in' to detect these private events."

Also, Dr. Donald Goodenough of New York State's Down-State Medical Center has found that some people dream so close to the waking stage, as shown by brain-wave recordings, that they think their dreams are only wakeful reveries. And here's a bizarre sidelight: You hear now and then of people who claim they never sleep. Actually, some scientists believe that such people sleep without knowing it - because they dream they're awake.

Torture Test: Going Without Dreams

If we dream so much, is there a reason for it? To find out, Dr. William Dement and other investigators at New York's Mount Sinai hospital put eight young men through what turned out to be a kind of torture test.

Night after night, as soon as the eight volunteers started to dream, as shown by eye movements, they were awakened. They were allowed to go back to sleep immediately after. So the dream-deprived sleepers got just as much sleep as sleepers in other experiments who were awakened only after finishing dreams. But during the day the dream-deprived - unlike the others became irritable and upset. They showed anxiety, had difficulty in concentrating. One left the study in apparent panic after three nights, and two others stopped short after four nights.

Even during the experiment, the sleepers had to be awakened increasingly on successive nights. They kept starting more and more dreams, trying to make up for the interrupted ones. One man, for example, began 7 dreams the first night, 10 the second, 17 the third, then 21, and finally 24 on the sixth and seventh nights. And immediately after the experiment was over, the men made up their dream quota by dreaming more than usual until they had regained their emotional composure.

"It is possible," says Dement, "that if the dream suppression were carried on long enough, a serious disruption of the personality would result." Adds Dr. Charles Fisher, a psychiatrist who checked on the dream-deprived men: "Dreaming permits each and every one of us to be quietly and safely insane every night of our lives."

How Dreams Help To Guard Our Sleep

Aside from allowing us to be insane in bed so we can be sane by day, dreams also protect our sleep. Sigmund Freud had that idea many years ago, and recent research show he was right.

Experimenters have rung bells, flashed lights, even splashed sleepers with water and found that often these disturbances are incorporated into dreams. The sound of an electric bell, for instance, becomes the ringing of a telephone or doorbell in a dream. When such a stimulus is woven into a dream, the sleeper goes right on sleeping undisturbed. Moreover, investigators have found that dreams have another protective action. "The dreamer can make all his wishes come true," says Dr. Kleitman. "Money, power, women, revenge, success - whatever he wants is his." Dreams it seems, are often so enjoyable that we try to hang onto them and, in the process, often go right on sleeping despite noises and other disturbances that would otherwise wake us.

Dreams Take Time To Happen

It used to be thought that a dream was over in a flash, that somehow, in the dream world, time was compressed and everything happened instantaneously. Not so.

Dreams run anywhere from nine minutes to an hour. And the course of time often appears to be about the same as in real life. Investigators have found, for example, that a dreamer takes as long to relate his dream as he spent in actually dreaming it. At the University of Chicago, when one man dreamed that he went to the hospital where he worked, performed a chore, and then came back to the Sleep Laboratory, an investigator personally went through the motions of going to the hospital, doing the chores, and then coming back. The time required corresponded to the length of the dream as shown by the dreamer's eye movements.

Dreams Come in Regular Cycles

We don't dream immediately upon going to sleep. First, for about 90 minutes, we drop into a deep dreamless sleep. Then we come up into a lighter stage of sleep and, with it, have a dream that averages about nine minutes in length. After that we go back into deep sleep again.

Successive dreams are increasingly lengthy. In an average night containing four dreams, the second runs about 19 minutes, the third about 24 minutes, and the fourth about 28 minutes. And the dreams come at fairly regular intervals - about every 90 minutes.

What's behind this spacing mechanism is unknown. But some scientists believe it's related to the cycle of rest and activity observed in infants. Infants generally sleep deeply for about an hour, then stir, either to awaken fully or to return to deep sleep again for an hour, after which the process is repeated. This cycle may increase with age, producing the 90-minute dreaming cycles seen in adults.

Can You Tell When And What Someone Else is Dreaming?

You can tell when by looking carefully at their eyes. If the eyeballs are moving beneath the lids, they are having a dream. Don't be misled by body movements. Actually, before a dream starts, there is great activity - movements of the arms or legs, or turning over in bed. But contrary to what most people think, once a dream gets under way, body movements stop, except for very minor ones such as finger twitching. At the end of the dream, the large body movements immediately begin again.

It's a fact, too, that mumbling or even distinct talking has nothing to do with dreams but usually occurs between episodes of dreaming.

As to what a dream is, you can't tell very much. You get some clues from the nature of the eye movements which indicate where the dreamer is looking. Up and down movements are connected with dreams involving climbing and similar vertical activities. Side to side movements characterize dreams that concern watching activities on a horizontal plane.

What Kinds of Dreams do People Have?

Almost a third are in color, the rest in black and white, with women and younger people tending to dream more in color than men and older people. But two-tone or otherwise, only a minority of dreams are loving or friendly. In 64 percent, Dr. Hall's studies indicate, hostility is the chief emotion. Actual murder turns up in only one of every 50 hostile dreams, but there's plenty of violence and violent talk.

Psychiatrists explain that this is so because in dreams we are not inhibited. We can express feelings we conceal from others and even deny to ourselves when awake - which makes dreams a good safety valve, and pleasurable as well.

Incidentally, in men's dreams, hostility is mostly directed against other men and friendliness is usually for women. But in women's dreams, friends and foes are of both sexes. From this some have concluded that while a man doesn't have much doubt about who his friends and enemies are, a woman never knows.

The Sameness of Dreams

Many people have certain dreams repeatedly. That, according to psychoanalytic studies, is because infantile wishes of childhood never disappear as long as they are suppressed. They keep working on the unconscious and stimulate the same dreams.

Also, according to Dr. Louis Robbins of the Menninger Foundation, everyone tends to suppress the same kind of infantile impulses - complete selfishness, for example. That's why there often are elements of similarity in the dreams of different people.

"Because of these similarities," Dr. Robbins adds, "some people believe that dreams, or parts of dreams, have fixed meanings and 'dream books' claim to enable anyone to interpret his dreams. The fact is, a black cat or an express train may have a different meaning for everyone." It takes an expert to interpret a dream - and the interpretation must be based on a lot of facts about the dreamer's life and experiences.

Who Dreams Most?

Generally, young people dream more than older people, women more than men, and those with high IQs more that those of lesser intelligence. These are the conclusions of studies such as those of Dr. Calvin S. Hall Jr., of Western Reserve University, who interviewed enough people to collect 10,000 dreams.

Do Dreams Foretell The Future

Julius Caesar's wife is said to have dreamed that he would be assassinated. Abraham Lincoln, according to Ward Lamon, his friend and biographer, not only dreamed in advance of his own assassination but of every important Northern victory during the Civil War.

Skeptics say that with 2.5 billion people in the world dreaming every night, it's only natural that occasionally one of them chances to dream of an incident that actually happens later on.

But some scientists think they now have a reason why dreams sometimes can be prophetic. Since dreams express hidden wishes, they say, a prophetic dream may merely show what the dreamer wants to happen in his life - and what he goes about achieving when awake even if he doesn't realize what he's doing. If he dreams, say, about a business or personal failure, and that actually happens later, it may be because he unconsciously wants the failure and does things to make it happen.

Dreams And Illness

Ever since Freud, who considered dreams to be "the royal road to the unconscious," psychoanalysts have probed patients' dreams to try to get at unconscious factors in emotional disorders. The trouble is that patients often forget dreams or have only very sketchy ideas about them by the time they climb onto the analytic couch.

Now it looks as if the new science of dreams may help psychiatry. In one experiment, patients under psychiatric treatment are spending occasional nights at a sleep laboratory where their sleep is monitored and they can be awakened immediately after each dream to record it on a dictating machine. The dreams are then sent to doctors for analysis.

Moreover, some medical men think the new dream science may have value in getting at the causes of a number of illnesses that tend to strike in the middle of the night, such as bronchial asthma, heart failure, and ulcer crisis. "Can it be," asks one physician, "that the occurrence of dreams may be responsible for such incidents?"

He may soon uncover clues. He proposes to add to the other electrodes for checking into dreams a few more for measuring such things as internal muscle changes and acid secretions during dreams."It may turn out," he remarks, "that we have to treat some asthma, coronary, and ulcer patients as psychological cases even when their trouble seems almost entirely organic. And we might use sedatives or drugs to keep the patient from reaching that distinctive stage in the sleep cycle that is essential to dreaming."

Whether or not this is practical remains to be determined. Since all of us apparently need dreams to keep us sane, stopping dreams as a means of treatment may prove to be a cure worse than the disease.

But dream science is still young. It's not even impossible that someday, instead of cutting off dreams entirely, scientists may find a specific pill to turn unhealthy dreams into healthy ones.

Is It Possible To Create The Perfect Dream?

Now here's something that definitely deserves the tag "incredibly interesting," psychologist Richard Wiseman has created an app to help influence your dreams

"*We have created a new way of carrying out mass participation experiments. We still know relatively little about the science of dreaming and this app may provide a real breakthrough in changing how we dream, and record and track those dreams.*"

At the time of writing over 13 million dreams have been recorded and Dream:ON is showing results for about 50% of users who try it for a several nights in a row.

If you would like to be a part of the world's largest dream experiment all you need to do is download the Dream:ON iPhone app via the following link.

itunes.apple.com/us/app/dream-on/id504521920

See link below for full details of the thinking and science behind the Dream:ON app

www.dreamonapp.com

18. JUST FOR FUN

"*What if everything is an illusion and nothing exists? In that case, I definitely overpaid for my carpet.*"

(Woody Allen)

If you study psychology people assume you know what they are thinking. Don't disillusion them; you can have a lot more fun that way.

How many psychologists does it take to change a light bulb?

Mind, Drugs and ID (but ironically not sex) are all words that can be formed from the letters in Sigmund Freud's name.

The majority of young psychology students are female; the majority of old psychology lecturers are male. Correlation study anyone!

Psychology experiments were way cooler back in the days when you could call people subjects and there was no such thing as ethics!

Psychology is listed on the Wikipedia Commonly misspelled words page (psycology).

Does the name Pavlov ring a bell?

Psychological testing being sensitively employed to help inform public awareness campaigns!

A couple of classic illusions for you. Look carefully, your visual system should start flipping between seeing a duck and a rabbit in the first image and an old women and a young girl in the second image.

A Freudian slip is when you say one thing but mean your mother!

"*I want to share something with you: The three little sentences that will get you through life. Number 1: Cover for me. Number 2: Oh, good idea, Boss! Number 3: It was like that when I got here.*" (Homer Simpson)

Did you misread the the first line? How about this line?

19. NEVER STOP LEARNING

"Learn as if you were going to live forever."

(Mahatma Gandhi)

I was the first person in my family to go to University. This meant there were no lofty expectations, no sense of pressure; just unconditional support and awareness that my loved ones would be proud of me whatever happened.

I couldn't really fail in this context and as soon as I realized that as with all things in life, the more you put in, the more you get out; learning became a pleasure rather than a means to an end.

Learning has provided me with opportunities that I would not have thought possible. It has taken me to new places around the world, it has given me work and lifestyle options, and it is even responsible for my wonderful family - I met my wife Louise at University and the rest as they say is history - now that's what I call the power of learning.

I sincerely believe that the best kind of learning is learning for learning's sake and there has never been a better time to do just that. As the World Wide Web has evolved it has revolutionized how we communicate, interact and acquire knowledge. This is particularly the case with the move towards what is known as web 2.0. Web 2.0 links people, it's a place where people contribute, share, collaborate and learn.

A quite brilliant example of web 2.0 is Coursera, a social entrepreneurship initiative where courses from top colleges are made available online, free, for anyone who wants to take them. How's this for a mission statement!

We envision a future where the top universities are educating not only thousands of students, but millions. Our technology enables the best professors to teach tens or hundreds of thousands of students.

Through this, we hope to give everyone access to the world-class education that has so far been available only to a select few. We want to empower people with education that will improve their lives, the lives of their families, and the communities they live in.

And how about this from Coursera Co-Founder Daphne Koller!

"*I'm a 3rd generation PhD, so it was expected that I would go to a good college. (My parents would likely have disowned me otherwise.) I was privileged to have the opportunity, and am passionate about making that available to others. I've been involved in teaching efforts at Stanford throughout my time as a faculty member, but now am committed to making great education available not just to those students lucky enough to attend Stanford, but to everyone around the world. Education should be a right, not a privilege, and I believe Coursera is a way to make that happen.*"

Take The World's Best Courses, Online, For Free

At the time of writing Coursera is offering 341 courses, from 62 universities. Here are just a few of the incredibly interesting courses you could be taking for free.

Social Psychology with Scott Plous, Professor of Psychology, Wesleyan University.

Ever wonder why people do what they do? This course offers some answers based on the latest research from social psychology. See following link for full course details.

www.coursera.org/course/socialpsychology

A Beginner's Guide to Irrational Behavior with Dan Ariely, Professor of Psychology and Behavioral Economics, Duke University.

Learn about some of the many ways in which people behave in less than rational ways, and how we might overcome these problems. See following link for full course details.

www.coursera.org/course/behavioralecon

Model Thinking with Scott E. Page, Professor of Complex Systems, Political Science, and Economics, University of Michigan.

Learn how to think with models and use them to make sense of the complex world around us. See following link for full course details.

www.coursera.org/course/modelthinking

Inspiring Leadership through Emotional Intelligence with Richard Boyatzis, Professor of Organizational Behavior, Psychology, and Cognitive Science at Case Western Reserve University.

Learn how emotional intelligence, hope, mindfulness, and compassion help a person reverse the damage of chronic stress and build great leadership relationships. See following link for full course details.

www.coursera.org/course/lead-ei

Sports and Society with Orin Starn, Professor and Chair of Cultural Anthropology, Duke University.

Learn about the role of sports around the world, and how the games we watch and play shape identity, culture, and society. See following link for full course details.

www.coursera.org/course/sports

Soul Beliefs: Causes and Consequences with Daniel M. Ogilvie Professor of Psychology, Rutgers University and Leonard W. Hamilton Professor of Psychology, Rutgers University.

Explore the causes and consequences of various beliefs about the soul. Topics such as the self, mind/body dualism, evolution, culture, death anxiety, afterlife, and religious and political conflict. See following link for full course details.

www.coursera.org/course/soulbeliefs

The Fiction of Relationship with Arnold Weinstein Professor of Comparative Literature, Brown University.

What is the nature of our relationship to others and the world? How can literature help us see these relationships more clearly? This course seeks to explore such questions through adventurous readings of ten great works of narrative fiction from the 18th to the 20th century. See following link for full course details.

www.coursera.org/course/relationship

Drugs And The Brain with Henry A. Lester Professor and Executive Officer for Neuroscience at the California Institute of Technology.

Learn about the neuroscience of drugs for therapy, for prevention, and for recreation and the prospects for new generations of medications in psychiatry, aging, and treatment of substance abuse. See following link for full course details.

www.coursera.org/course/drugsandbrain

Know Thyself with Mitchell Green Professor of Philosophy, University of Virginia.

Investigate the nature and limits of self-knowledge from the viewpoints of philosophy, psychoanalysis, experimental psychology, neuroscience, aesthetics, and Buddhism. See following link for full course details.

www.coursera.org/course/knowthyself

I'm certainly going to be signing-up for some of these great free courses; I hope you will be too.

"*That is what learning is. You suddenly understand something you've understood all your life, but in a new way.*"

(Doris Lessing)

20. PSYCHOLOGY GETS POLITICAL

In 1943 William Donovan the director of the Office of Strategic Services (the forerunner to the CIA) approached Harvard psychologist Walter Langer and asked him to construct a psychological profile of Adolf Hitler.

Despite his reservations regarding the reliability of the data upon which his analysis would be based, Langer set about this unprecedented task by putting together a team of psychologists and researchers. Langer and his team had just five months to produce their findings, in which time they interviewed key informants who knew Hitler personally as well as drawing upon over 1000 pages of background research from a document known as The Hitler Source Book.

Langer stated that his analysis was an attempt to process contradictory, conflicting and unreliable material concerning Hitler into meaningful categories which would be helpful to policy-makers and those engaged in counter-propaganda; and presented his psychological profile within five specific sections in order to understand Hitler as a person and the motivations underlying his actions. The five profile sections were:

1. Hitler as he believes himself to be.

2. Hitler as the German people know him.

3. Hitler as his associates know him.

4. Hitler as he knows himself.

5. Psychological analysis and reconstruction.

Freudianism at its Height

In constructing his psychological analysis of Hitler, Langer drew heavily upon the ideas of Sigmund Freud, most notably Freud's ideas concerning the developmental influence of early childhood experiences. As such Langer's report provides the reader with a fascinating window into the mechanics of Freudian analysis. Among the issues discussed within this paradigm were:

Hitler's character as influenced by his father.

Hitler's mother and her influence.

Hitler's attitude towards love, women and marriage.

Hitler's early conflicts expressed in symbolic form.

The Messiah Complex.

Desire for immortality.

Sexual development.

One extremely prophetic extract from Langer's analysis occurs when addressing Hitler's probable behavior in the future, suggesting that he might commit suicide.

"*This is the most plausible outcome. Not only has he frequently threatened to commit suicide, but from what we know of his psychology it is the most likely possibility. It is probably true that he has an inordinate fear of death, but being an hysteric he could undoubtedly screw himself up into the super-man character and perform the deed. In all probability, however, it would not be a simple suicide. He has too much of the dramatic for that and since immortality is one of his dominant motives we can imagine that he would stage the most dramatic and effective death scene he could possibly think of. He knows how to bind the people to him and if he cannot have the bond in life he will certainly do his utmost to achieve it in death.*"

Political Profiling

Without doubt the greatest legacy of Langer's report was the influence it had on the field of political profiling. Dr Jerrold Post cites Langer's analysis of Hitler as the inspiration for the profiling unit he established at the CIA in the 1970s; a unit which would go on to profile every major world leader up to and including Saddam Hussein.

In discussing Langer's psychological profile of Hitler during an interview with the BBC, Post stated:

"*We must understand the leaders we are contending with - you can't deter optimally a leader you don't understand - and to relegate be it a Hitler or a Joseph Stalin or a Saddam Hussein to a crazy evil madman really degrades our capacity to deal with them optimally because we're not thinking about what pushes them, what makes them tick.*"

While the value of political profiling remains open to question, the seminal importance of Langer's psychological study of Adolf Hitler in influencing its development is not.

If you would like to read Langer's psychological profile of Hitler in full it is available both on the kindle and in paperback format. See following links for full details.

www.amazon.com/dp/B004TSPFLS (Kindle version)

http://goo.gl/zlpqm (Paperback Version)

21. A QUICK GUIDE TO FORENSIC PSYCHOLOGY

This chapter concerns a type of psychology I'm personally most familiar with. In 2000 I was involved in collaborative research with a number of forensic odontologists (dentists) in the UK, US and Canada, and it was during this time that I began to pursue an interest in forensic psychology.

Following a mass casualty incident e.g., a plane crash, forensic odontologists undertake body identification work by analyzing dental remains. Part of the research I carried out examined the emotional and psychological impact of conducting work of this kind. (Webb DA, Sweet D, Pretty IA. The emotional and psychological impact of mass casualty incidents on forensic odontologists. J Forensic Sci 2002;47(3):539-541.)

I also got to explore behavioral aspects of biting behavior within the context of a criminal investigation due to the fact that human bitemarks are often found on the victims of violent and sexual crimes, i.e., serial murder, rape, and child abuse. (Webb DA, Sweet D, Hinman DL, Pretty IA. Forensic implications of biting behavior: a conceptually underdeveloped area of investigation. J Forensic Sci 2002;47(1):103-106.)

In the process of researching these topics I was extremely fortunate to be able to draw on the experience and expertise of my co-authors. Dr. David Sweet and Dr. Iain A. Pretty are eminent figures within the field of legal dentistry and at the time Dayle Hinman was Statewide Coordinator of the Criminal Assessment/Profiling Program, Florida Department of Law Enforcement. Conducting research with professionals who operate under the umbrella of forensic science meant that I had the opportunity to attend a number of forensic conferences, the majority of which had a behavioral science or forensic psychology section.

My general interest in forensic psychology turned to academic interest when as a University lecturer I had the opportunity to write and deliver an undergraduate course in forensic psychology.

When my students arrived for their first lecture, I would always start by asking them to write down an answer to the question, what is forensic psychology? The reason I did this was because students were always strongly advised to speak to the course leader before choosing a particular study option and in all the time I ran the course I never had a single student come and see me in advance.

So Why The No Show?

The most common reason given by students was that they felt they already knew what forensic psychology was all about. Or so they thought!

I mentioned that at the start of the first lecture I would give students a few minutes to write down an answer to the question "what is forensic psychology?" What I didn't mention, however, is that after a couple of minutes I would ask for their attention and apologize for forgetting to tell them that they weren't allowed to use the words serial killers, criminal profiling or Silence of the Lambs in their answer. It was usually at this point that most of the students stopped writing.

A Divided Discipline

The first thing to bear in mind when addressing the question what is forensic psychology is that even psychologists in the field are divided as to the answer

Gudjonsson and Haward note that the division of criminological and legal psychology within the British Psychological Society debated for twenty years over whether their members should be entitled to call themselves Chartered Forensic Psychologists.

So What Was The problem?

The main bone of contention was that members hailed from a wide range of disciplines e.g. psychologists in the prison/correctional services, clinical psychologists in special hospitals and the psychiatric services, educational psychologists, industrial/organizational/occupation psychologists, academics researchers etc. It was, therefore, difficult to state what the boundaries were when discussing the practice of forensic psychology. However, it is important to note that all of these areas fall under the umbrella of forensic psychology because their work, expert knowledge or research activity is somehow connected with the law.

This legal connection makes sense when you consider that the word forensic comes from the Latin *forensis*, which literally means appertaining to the forum, specifically the imperial court of Rome. So in essence the debate as to what forensic psychology is, and what forensic psychology is not, rests primarily on the nature of psychology's relationship with the legal system.

Let me give you an example. Imagine two psychologists meet at a conference and they begin talking about the work they do.

The first psychologist tells the second that she recently gave expert testimony in court arguing that in her opinion the defendant in a murder case was criminally insane. The judge and jury agreed and having been found guilty on the grounds of diminished responsibility the defendant was sent to a secure psychiatric unit.

Now there's a coincidence the second psychologist says I work in the unit where they sent him.

So here you have a situation where two psychologists are linked to the legal system by way of a legal decision. You could argue, therefore, that both deserve to be seen as engaging in Forensic Psychology. However, there's a crucial difference.

The first psychologist actually helped inform the legal decision based on her psychological knowledge and expertise. The second psychologist's involvement on the other hand arose as a consequence of a legal decision that she had no direct involvement with.

My preferred definition of forensic psychology acknowledges this key distinction.

"*That branch of applied psychology which is concerned with the collection, examination and presentation of evidence for judicial purposes*" (Haward 1981).

If you adopt this definition, the answer to the question what is forensic psychology becomes clear, because you are stating categorically that Forensic Psychology relates to - "*The provision of psychological information for the purpose of facilitating a legal decision.* " (Blackburn 1996). So in the case of our two psychologists, strictly speaking only the first can be said to be engaged in Forensic Psychology. Please note though that there is also a school of thought which suggests that any activity that links psychology to the law deserves to be described as forensic.

The first recorded example of a psychologist acting as an expert witness in a court of law was in 1896 when Albert Von Schrenk-Notzing testified at the trial of a man accused of murdering three women. Drawing on research into memory and suggestibility Schrenk-Notzing argued that pre-trial publicity meant that witnesses would not be able to distinguish between what they actually saw and what had been reported in the press. A perceptual error coined retroactive memory falsification.

The interesting thing about this case is not only its importance in the history of forensic psychology but also the fact that over a century later similar psychological evidence is still being debated in court. A very similar argument to that put forward by Schrenk-Notzing was raised during the trial of the infamous mass murderer Dr Harold Shipman.

Other Historical Landmarks

In terms of a tangible landmark in the history of forensic psychology the most significant development was the founding of the first psychological laboratory in 1879 by Wilhelm Wundt in Leipzig Germany.

Wilhelm Wundt championed and refined the experimental method within psychology. This rigorous methodology provided the framework for a whole host of applied psychological investigations, among them certain legal issues. For instance, in 1895 Cattell conducted experiments into the nature of testimony and in doing so highlighted the effects of situational and individual differences.

Hugo Munsterberg

I have given Hugo Munsterberg his own sub-heading because I must confess to being a real fan. Not only did he boast a great name and an outrageous moustache but he was also a passionate advocate of forensic psychology.

An engaging and controversial figure, Munsterberg studied under Wundt at Leipzg before moving to the United States in 1892 to set up an experimental laboratory at Harvard, the principal aim of which was to introduce applied psychology into the courtroom.

Initially, Munsterberg's ideas were not taken seriously and were largely ignored by the legal profession much to his obvious annoyance.

"*The lawyer and the judge and the juryman are sure that they do not need the experimental psychologist. They do not wish to see that in this field preeminently applied experimental psychology has made strong strides, led by Binet, Stern, Lipmann, Jung, Wertheimer, Gross, Sommer, Aschaffenburg, and other scholars. They go on thinking that their legal instinct and their common sense supplies them with all that is needed and somewhat more; and if the time is ever to come when even the jurist is to show some concession to the spirit of modern psychology, public opinion will have to exert some pressure. Just in the line of the law it therefore seems necessary not to rely simply on the technical statements of scholarly treatises, but to carry the discussion in the most popular form possible before the wider tribunal of the general reader.*

With this aim in mind while working at a treatise on "Applied Psychology," which is to cover the whole ground with technical detail I have written the following popular sketches, which select only a few problems in which psychology and law come in contact. They deal essentially with the mind of the witness on the witness stand; only the last, on the prevention of crime, takes another direction. I have not touched so far the psychology of the attorney, of the judge, or of the jury problems which lend themselves to very interesting experimental treatment. Even the psychology of the witness is treated in no way exhaustively; my only purpose is to turn the attention of serious men to an absurdly neglected field which demands the full attention of the social community."

Completely undeterred by the apparent lack of interest in what he had to say, Munsterberg set about promoting and advancing the field of forensic psychology.

He conducted research into witness memory, false confessions and the role of hypnosis in court and one of his earliest experiments tested subjects' ability to discriminate between sounds heard in quick succession.

Almost sixty years later his findings were included as part of the preparation for the trial (which for obvious reasons never actually took place) of Lee Harvey Oswald to help address the question of how many shots had been fired during the assassination of President Kennedy.

If you would like to read a free full-text copy of Hugo Munsterberg's landmark publication: On The Witness Stand: Essays on Psychology & Crime - you can do so via the following link

www.all-about-forensic-psychology.com/hugo-munsterberg.html

Psychometric Assessment

In 1889 Alfred Binet co-founded the first psychological laboratory in France. Having studied medicine and law he was interested in how psychology could be applied within the legal system, particularly in relation to witness testimony. However, it was Binet's work into intellectual assessment that was to have the greatest forensic impact. Working alongside Theodore Simon, he developed the first psychometric test of intelligence, the principles of which proved the basis for later forensic assessment.

In the United States the Wechsler Intelligence test for children was regularly employed as part of proceedings within juvenile court. Group testing became extremely popular, particularly within the armed services as a way of selecting recruits and before long objective tests were being employed across a host of professions and for a variety of purposes as a means of measuring behavioral traits, skills, attitudes etc. Significantly for the practice of forensic psychology this included the judiciary who began allowing test results to be presented as evidence in court.

Recent History

In the last thirty years or so a number of high profile legal issues have been addressed by psychologists. These include the issue of recovered memories in child abuse cases, disputed confessions and Post Traumatic Stress Disorder. More recently it has been the development of interviewing techniques such as the cognitive interview which has underlined the legal application of psychology.

What Does A Forensic Psychologist Do?

This really depends on the experience, background, working environment, psychological/forensic knowledge etc; of the forensic psychologist in question.

It is probably better, therefore, to ask what does this particular forensic psychologist do?

Learn More

For free and comprehensive information on forensic psychology visit my forensic psychology website. Definitions, history, criminal profiling, forensic psychology theory and practice, careers and degree options are just some of the many topics covered in detail.

www.all-about-forensic-psychology.com

22. PSYCHOLOGY MOVIES

"Film is more than the twentieth-century art. It's another part of the twentieth-century mind."

(Don Delillo)

(Photo Credit ToastyKen via Flickr Creative Commons)

The inextricable link between movies and psychology is an obvious one when you consider that when you watch a film you are invariably observing human behavior in its many ways shapes and forms.

Movies that deal specifically with psychological issues and topics have been a mainstay of the film industry, however, concern has been raised that the portrayal of psychology in general along with that of psychologists and psychological disorders has been far from accurate on the whole.

Indeed, such was the concern surrounding psychology movies that in 1998 members of the media psychology division of the American Psychological Society established a Media Watch Committee to examine the way psychologists, particularly therapists were portrayed in movies, as well as television shows and books.

Become A Psychology Movies Film Critic

Next time you watch a movie with a psychological theme; why not reflect upon and research whether it was an accurate portrayal. It's one of the most enjoyable ways I know of learning more about psychology.

Not sure what to watch?

I recently ran a *Best Psychology Movies* poll on the All About Psychology Facebook page. (www.facebook.com/psychologyonline) Over 2000 people voted and the top ten results were as follows (description of each film provided courtesy of Wikipedia.)

1. A Beautiful Mind

A Beautiful Mind is a 2001 American biographical drama film based on the life of John Nash, a Nobel Laureate in Economics. The film was directed by Ron Howard, from a screenplay written by Akiva Goldsman. It was inspired by a bestselling, Pulitzer Prize-nominated 1998 book of the same name by Sylvia Nasar. The film stars Russell Crowe, along with Ed Harris, Jennifer Connelly, Paul Bettany and Christopher Plummer in supporting roles. The story begins in the early years of a young prodigy named John Nash. Early in the film, Nash begins developing paranoid schizophrenia and endures delusional episodes while painfully watching the loss and burden his condition brings on his wife and friends.

2. The Silence of The Lambs

The Silence of the Lambs is a 1991 American thriller directed by Jonathan Demme and starring Jodie Foster, Anthony Hopkins, Ted Levine, and Scott Glenn. It is based on Thomas Harris' 1988 novel of the same name, his second to feature Hannibal Lecter, a brilliant psychiatrist and cannibalistic serial killer. In the film, Clarice Starling, a young U.S. Federal Bureau of Investigation trainee, seeks the advice of the imprisoned Dr. Lecter to apprehend another serial killer, known only as "Buffalo Bill."

3. Shutter Island

Shutter Island is a 2010 American psychological thriller film directed by Martin Scorsese. The film is based on Dennis Lehane's 2003 novel of the same name. Leonardo DiCaprio stars as U.S. Marshal Edward "Teddy" Daniels, who is investigating a psychiatric facility on the titular island.

4. Black Swan

Black Swan is a 2010 American psychological thriller directed by Darren Aronofsky and starring Natalie Portman, Vincent Cassel, and Mila Kunis. The plot revolves around a production of Tchaikovsky's Swan Lake ballet by a prestigious New York City company. The production requires a ballerina to play the innocent and fragile White Swan, for which the committed dancer Nina (Portman) is a perfect fit, as well as the dark and sensual Black Swan, which are qualities embodied by the new arrival Lily (Kunis). Nina is overwhelmed by a feeling of immense pressure when she finds herself competing for the part, causing her to lose her tenuous grip on reality and descend into a living nightmare.

5. Fight Club

Fight Club is a 1999 American film based on the 1996 novel of the same name by Chuck Palahniuk. The film was directed by David Fincher and stars Edward Norton, Brad Pitt, and Helena Bonham Carter. Norton plays the unnamed protagonist, an "everyman" who is discontented with his white-collar job. He forms a "fight club" with soap maker Tyler Durden, played by Pitt, and becomes embroiled in a relationship with him and a dissolute woman, Marla Singer, played by Bonham Carter.

6. One Flew Over the Cuckoo's Nest

One Flew Over the Cuckoo's Nest is a 1975 drama film directed by Miloš Forman and based on the 1962 novel of the same name by Ken Kesey. Set in an Oregon psychiatric hospital, the narrative serves as a study of the institutional processes and the human mind as well as a critique of Behaviorism and a celebration of humanistic principles.

7. Eternal Sunshine of the Spotless Mind

Eternal Sunshine of the Spotless Mind is a 2004 American romantic drama science fiction film about an estranged couple who have each other erased from their memories. Scripted by Charlie Kaufman and directed by the French director, Michel Gondry, the film stars an ensemble cast that includes Jim Carrey, Kate Winslet, Kirsten Dunst, Mark Ruffalo, Tom Wilkinson, Elijah Wood, Jane Adams, and David Cross. The title of the film is taken from the poem Eloisa to Abelard by Alexander Pope, the story of a tragic love affair, where forgetfulness became the heroine's only comfort.

8. Catch Me if You Can

Catch Me If You Can is a 2002 American biographical crime film based on the life of Frank Abagnale, who, before his 19th birthday, successfully performed cons worth millions of dollars by posing as a Pan American World Airways pilot, a Georgia doctor, and a Louisiana parish prosecutor. The film was directed by Steven Spielberg and stars Leonardo DiCaprio and Tom Hanks, with Christopher Walken, Amy Adams, Martin Sheen, and Nathalie Baye in supporting roles.

9. Good Will Hunting

Good Will Hunting is a 1997 American drama film directed by Gus Van Sant and starring Matt Damon, Robin Williams, Ben Affleck, Minnie Driver, and Stellan Skarsgard. Written by Affleck and

Damon, and with Damon in the title role, the film follows 20-year-old South Boston laborer Will Hunting, an unrecognized genius who, as part of a deferred prosecution agreement after assaulting a police officer, becomes a patient of a therapist (Williams) and studies advanced mathematics with a renowned professor (Skarsgard). Through his therapy sessions, Will re-evaluates his relationships with his best friend (Affleck), his girlfriend (Driver), and himself, facing the significant task of thinking about his future.

10. Girl, Interrupted

Girl, Interrupted is a 1999 drama film, and an adaptation of Susanna Kaysen's 1993 memoir of the same name. The film chronicles Kaysen's 18-month stay at a mental institution. Directed by James Mangold, the film stars Winona Ryder as Kaysen, with a supporting cast that includes Angelina Jolie, Brittany Murphy, Whoopi Goldberg and Vanessa Redgrave.

Want more suggestions?

When I posted the results of the psychology movies poll it generated lots of debate as to what other films should have included. Here is a selection of some of the comments made.

They missed one of the most brilliant movies from, I think 1975. Three faces of Eve! Absolutely brilliant! Hard to come by, but really worth it. (Tania Marisa Lara Bocher)

There's something about Kevin... Great film about what happens when a child is neglected and insecurely attached to his mother! (Selina Hossain)

Let's not forget Robert Redford's directorial debut with "Ordinary People" (1980). Real people issues ... family system imbalance and the struggles to maintain appearances when the world is crumbling around them, and yet, all are in states of denial and emotional turmoil inside. Excellent movie! (James Coop)

I'm surprised that Donnie Darko is not on the list. However, "The Dark

Knight" while a wonderful action film had some overriding psychological themes. There's the dual minded hero, the socially accepted hero who is dual minded as well and then there is the obvious mentally unstable villain, who may not completely be mentally unstable but a raving social challenger. We could all have a field day with this movie - ok, well, the Joker was crazy - but you all can see where I'm going with this. (Christina Abrams)

The Snake Pit, about a woman in a psychiatric hospital in the late 1940s. Very interesting stuff which makes me glad our hospitals aren't like that anymore. (Katherine Norton)

A film I thought was good is 'The Handmaid's Tale'. The film comes under Self and Identity in Social Psychology. (Stephanie Gordon)

"12 angry men" is a great movie. The newer version of the movie is more diverse and inclusive. The movie depicts the power of perception, because action is the interpreter of thoughts. The 12 jurors deliberated based on personal life experiences and interests, and not on facts. Great movie. (J. Ibeh Agbanyim)

P.S. I'd also recommend one my all time favorite films *Being John Malkovich*, I could try and explain the plot but it is one of those films where it is probably best just to watch it.

Psychology Movie Trailer Playlist

Based on the poll mentioned above and the additional suggestions put forward in response, I have started work on a movie trailer video playlist featuring films with a psychological aspect to them. See following link for details.

www.youtube.com/playlist?list=PL7249F07CEEDD1F1E

23. INTERESTING ARTICLES

A very exciting development within the world of academia has been the move towards open access publishing; an initiative whereby full text, quality controlled scientific and scholarly journal articles are made freely available.

Below you will find details of some very interesting open access psychology related articles. To access any of the featured articles in full simply visit the appropriate link. (Internet connection required.)

Self-Guided Psychological Treatment for Depressive Symptoms: A Meta-Analysis. Pim Cuijpers, Tara Donker, Robert Johansson, David C. Mohr, Annemieke van Straten and Gerhard Andersson

A number of trials have examined the effects of self-guided psychological intervention, without any contact between the participants and a therapist or coach. The results and sizes of these trials have been mixed. This is the first quantitative meta-analysis, aimed at organizing and evaluating the literature, and estimating effect size. We found evidence that self-guided psychological treatment has a small but significant effect on participants with increased levels of depressive symptomatology.

www.plosone.org/article/info%3Adoi%2F10.1371%2Fjournal.pone.0021274

Applications of lucid dreams: An online study. Melanie Schädlich and Daniel Erlacher

In a lucid dream the dreamer is aware of the dream state and can influence the dream content and events. The goal of this study was to investigate some applications of lucid dreaming.

http://archiv.ub.uni-heidelberg.de/ojs/index.php/IJoDR/article/view/9505

You do not talk about Fight Club if you do not notice Fight Club: Inattentional blindness for a simulated real-world assault. Christopher F Chabris, Adam Weinberger, Matthew Fontaine and Daniel J Simons

Inattentional blindness—the failure to see visible and otherwise salient events when one is paying attention to something else—has been proposed as an explanation for various real-world events. In one such event, a Boston police officer chasing a suspect ran past a brutal assault and was prosecuted for perjury when he claimed not to have seen it. However, there have been no experimental studies of inattentional blindness in real-world conditions. We simulated the Boston incident by having subjects run after a confederate along a route near which three other confederates staged a fight. At night only 35% of subjects noticed the fight; during the day 56% noticed. We manipulated the attentional load on the subjects and found that increasing the load significantly decreased noticing. These results provide evidence that inattentional blindness can occur during real-world situations, including the Boston case.

http://i-perception.perceptionweb.com/journal/I/article/i0436

Belonging to Tomorrow: An Overview of Procrastination. Brian A. Wilson and Tuyen D. Nguyen

Available material indicates that the formal study of procrastination is a relatively recent occurrence. This literature review examines the work of some of the most prominent researchers in this field. This paper will examine the underlying causes of procrastination as delineated by the most current research. In addition, it will explore the hypothesis that procrastination exists on a scale, and that in its most elevated state can have severe, substantial and lasting consequences. Finally, this paper will review some methods for blunting the impact of procrastination, and briefly examine what lies ahead in the study of this condition.

www.ccsenet.org/journal/index.php/ijps/article/view/15463/10590

Reaction Times and Deception - the Lying Constant. Martin R. Sheridan and Kenneth A. Flowers

The cognitive theory of lie detection suggests that it takes longer on average to formulate a deliberately false response than a truthful one because it requires the truth to first be known and then altered, adding an extra component to the response process. This concept was upheld in a modified form in three experiments where subjects indicated as quickly as possible whether presented numbers were higher or lower than a given standard number, and to "lie" (give the wrong answer deliberately) on half the trials. Results suggested that lying adds a constant additional time to reaction times (RTs) independently of other factors such as the complexity of the cognitive task or method of response. Additionally, true Yes RTs were shorter than true No ones, producing an interaction with the lying constant such that RTs could reliably distinguish truth from lies for Yes responses but not so easily for No responses.

www.ccsenet.org/journal/index.php/ijps/article/view/6498/6362

Young Children Consider Merit when Sharing Resources with Others. Patricia Kanngiesser and Felix Warneken

Merit is a key principle of fairness: rewards should be distributed according to how much someone contributed to a task. Previous research suggests that children have an early ability to take merit into account in third-party situations but that merit-based sharing in first-party contexts does not emerge until school-age. Here we provide evidence that three- and five-year-old children already use merit to share resources with others, even when sharing is costly for the child.

www.plosone.org/article/info%3Adoi%2F10.1371%2Fjournal.pone.0043979

Improving Students' Learning With Effective Learning Techniques: Promising Directions From Cognitive and Educational Psychology. John Dunlosky, Katherine A. Rawson, Elizabeth J. Marsh, Mitchell J. Nathan, and Daniel T. Willingham

Many students are being left behind by an educational system that some people believe is in crisis. Improving educational outcomes will require efforts on many fronts, but a central premise of this monograph is that one part of a solution

involves helping students to better regulate their learning through the use of effective learning techniques.

Fortunately, cognitive and educational psychologists have been developing and evaluating easy-to-use learning techniques that could help students achieve their learning goals. In this monograph, we discuss 10 learning techniques in detail and offer recommendations about their relative utility.

http://psi.sagepub.com/content/14/1/4.full

The Eyes Don't Have It: Lie Detection and Neuro-Linguistic Programming. Richard Wiseman, Caroline Watt2, Leanne ten Brinke, Stephen Porter, Sara-Louise Couper and Calum Rankin

Proponents of Neuro-Linguistic Programming (NLP) claim that certain eye-movements are reliable indicators of lying. According to this notion, a person looking up to their right suggests a lie whereas looking up to their left is indicative of truth telling. Despite widespread belief in this claim, no previous research has examined its validity. In Study 1 the eye movements of participants who were lying or telling the truth were coded, but did not match the NLP patterning. In Study 2 one group of participants were told about the NLP eye-movement hypothesis whilst a second control group were not. Both groups then undertook a lie detection test. No significant differences emerged between the two groups. Study 3 involved coding the eye movements of both liars and truth tellers taking part in high profile press conferences. Once again, no significant differences were discovered. Taken together the results of the three studies fail to support the claims of NLP. The theoretical and practical implications of these findings are discussed.

www.plosone.org/article/info%3Adoi%2F10.1371%2Fjournal.pone.0040259

24. MAXIMS TO LIVE YOUR LIFE BY

In 1905 legendary psychologist William James published a tribute to the memory of his very good friend and eminent philosopher Thomas Davidson.

Within his tribute James refers to a letter Davidson wrote in which Davidson summed up the results of his own experience of life by way of a series of twenty maxims. These were among his wonderful pearls of wisdom.

Rely upon your own energies, and do not wait for, or depend on other people.

Cling with all your might to your own highest ideals, and do not be led astray by such vulgar aims as wealth, position, popularity. Be yourself.

Your worth consists in what you are, and not in what you have. What you are will show in what you do.

Never fret, repine, or envy. Do not make yourself unhappy by comparing your circumstances with those of more fortunate people; but make the most of the opportunities you have. Employ profitably every moment.

Associate with the noblest people you can find; read the best books; live with the mighty. But learn to be happy alone.

Do not believe that all greatness and heroism are in the past. Learn to discover princes, prophets, heroes, and saints among the people about you. Be assured they are there.

Cultivate ideal friendships, and gather into an intimate circle all your acquaintances who are hungering for truth and right.

Do not shrink from any useful or kindly act, however hard or repellent it may be. The worth of acts is measured by the spirit in which they are performed.

If a thousand plans fail, be not disheartened. As long as your purposes are right, you have not failed.

Examine yourself every night, and see whether you have progressed in knowledge, sympathy, and helpfulness during the day. Count every day a loss in which no progress has been made.

Seek enjoyment in energy, not in dalliance. Our worth is measured solely by what we do.

Let not your goodness be professional; let it be the simple, natural outcome of your character. Therefore cultivate character.

If you do wrong, say so, and make what atonement you can. That is true nobleness. Have no moral debts.

Wear no placards, within or without. Be human fully.

25. HONORARY PSYCHOLOGISTS

This chapter plays tribute to those individuals who found fame outside the discipline of psychology but still made a significant contribution towards it.

Sir Francis Galton

A highly regarded Victorian polymath, Galton published hundreds of works across a remarkable range of topics. For instance, he was the first person to study the science of fingerprints and was also the first person to produce a public weather map in 1875.

Although Galton's work on inheritance and the concept of eugenics is probably his most lasting and controversial legacy; Steve Jones professor of genetics at University College London notes that "*the most important part of Galton's work had nothing to do with eugenics, for he was one of the first to realize that science - biology as much as physics - needs maths rather than words. He was one of the founders of the science of statistics, and he measured many things.*"

He also made lots of interesting, quirky and sometimes downright bizarre contributions to psychology. For example, here is a short article by Galton first published in psychological review in 1894.

Arithmetic By Smell

It seems worthwhile to put a few simple experiments on record, which I made for my own satisfaction a few months ago, in order to assure myself that arithmetic may be performed by the sole medium of imaginary smells, just as by imaginary figures or sounds. I had first to familiarize myself with a variety of scents, for which purpose the following arrangement was provided. Each scent was poured profusely upon cotton wool, loosely packed in a brass tube 8/4 inch in outside diameter, which had a nozzle at one of its ends. The other wide-open end of the brass tube was pushed into a tightly fitting piece of caoutchouc tubing, 4 and a half inches long, and the opposite end of the tubing was stopped with a cork. Whenever the tubing is grasped by the hand, a whiff of scented air is forced through the nozzle; when the grasp is relaxed, fresh air enters through the nozzle and passing through the wool becomes quickly impregnated with scent. The apparatus is then ready to be used again. Whiffs of scented air may thus be sent out four or five times in moderately quick succession and be almost equally odorous throughout.

In using the apparatus, I begin by breathing out slowly through the nose, to prevent any scent from being prematurely perceived; in the mean time the nozzle is brought below the nostrils. Then I simultaneously give a sudden grasp and a sudden sniff up. A separate apparatus is used for each scent. They are made as alike as possible, and are scarcely distinguishable; nevertheless it is well to operate with the eyes shut. The scents chiefly used were peppermint, camphor, carbolic acid, ammonia, and aniseed. I taught myself to associate two whiffs of peppermint with one whiff of camphor; three of peppermint with one of carbolic acid, and so on.

Next, I practised at some small sums in addition; at first with the scents themselves, and afterwards altogether with the imagination of them. There was not the slightest difficulty in banishing all visual and auditory images from the mind, leaving nothing in the consciousness besides real or imaginary scents. In this way, without, it is true, becoming very apt at the process, I convinced myself of the possibility of doing sums in simple addition with considerable speed and accuracy solely by means of imaginary scents. Further than this I did not go, so far as addition was concerned. It seemed a serious waste of time to continue the experiments further, because their difficulty and complexity rapidly increased. There were also provoking lapses of memory. For instance, at the present moment, having discontinued the experiments for three months, I find my old lessons almost wholly forgotten. Few persons appreciate the severity of the task imposed on children in making them learn the simple multiplication table, with its 81 pairs of values each associated with a third value. No wonder that they puzzle over it for months, notwithstanding the remarkable receptivity of their fresh brains. I did not attempt multiplication by smell.

Subtraction succeeded as well as addition. I did not go so far as to associate separate scents with the attitudes of mind severally appropriate to subtraction and addition, but determined by my ordinary mental processes which attitude to assume, before isolating myself in the world of scents.

Few experiments were made with taste. Salt, sugar, citric acid, and quinine seemed suitable for the purpose, and there appeared to be little difficulty in carrying on the experiments to a sufficient extent to show that arithmetic by taste was as feasible as arithmetic by smell.

Charles Darwin

In addition to his groundbreaking work within the field of biology and evolutionary theory, it turns out that Charles Darwin also conducted pioneering work within psychology; particularly in relation to the expression of emotion.

As a result of some wonderful academic archival research, Professor of Neurology, Peter Snyder uncovered details of an experiment conducted by Darwin which was one of the very first studies on how people recognize emotion in faces. This work arose from his correspondence with French physician Guillaume-Benjamin-Amand Duchenne who suggested that at least 60 discrete emotions - all with their own dedicated group of facial muscles - could be discerned from the human face.

Darwin was not convinced, believing instead that facial muscles worked in tandem to produce just a few universal emotional expressions. To test his hypothesis, Darwin conducted a single-blind study at his home in England. Darwin's house guests were randomly shown 11 of the picture slides Duchenne had employed in his research. Darwin asked each respondent to state what emotion the person in the picture slide appeared to be displaying.

During his archival research of Darwin's work on emotion professor Snyder found handwritten notes and data tables which showed that there was almost universal agreement among Darwin's respondents regarding emotions such as happiness, sadness, fear and surprise.

Specific Contributions

In 1909 the psychologist James Rowland Angell wrote the following account of the influence of Darwin on Psychology.

Darwinism has never been a really vital issue in psychology. Occasionally a theologian or a naturalist has inveighed against the Darwinian theory of mental evolution, but the psychologists as such have rarely uttered a protest. In view of the storm of vituperative scientific criticism precipitated by the publication of the Origin of Species, this fact is distinctly significant. Indeed, so much a matter of course have the essential Darwinian conceptions become, that one is in danger of assuming fallaciously that Darwinism has no important bearing on psychology. How Darwin's radical theories succeeded in gaining such easy access to the psychological sanctuary is a matter of distinct interest upon which a few speculative comments may be made.

It must be borne in mind, then, that Darwin's most revolutionary ideas on mental evolution did not appear until the publication of the Descent of Man in 1871. This was nearly thirty years after Weber's epoch-making experiments on sensations, almost a score of years after the appearance of Lotze's medical psychology, sixteen years after the issuance of Spencer's evolutionary psychology and Bain's work on the Senses and Intellect, with its excellent presentation of the facts of nervous organization, eleven years after Fechner's publication of the Psychophysik, nine years after the first edition of

Helmholtz's Sensations of Tone and seven years after his Physiological Optics. It was only three years in advance of the first edition of Wundt's Physiological Psychology. There had thus been rapidly growing during the preceding thirty years a disposition to view mental life as intimately connected with physiological processes, as capable of investigation along experimental and physiological lines, and finally as susceptible of explanation in an evolutionary manner. Moreover, by the time the Descent of Man was published the weight of scientific authority, so heavily against Darwin at the time of the publication of the Origin of Species in 1859, had swung unmistakably to his support.

Another circumstance of probably more than negligible moment is found in the fact that the major interest of many psychologists has always been in the more narrowly analytical problems of mind. On these problems Darwinism has had little immediate bearing and has exercised only the smallest fructifying influence. Its contentions have seemed, therefore, to demand no very vigorous partisanship either one way or the other.

The effect of certain philosophic tendencies ought, no doubt, to be added to this brief survey of contributory influences, but the considerations already offered are probably sufficient to indicate in part, at least, why the publication of the doctrines of mental evolution expounded in the Descent of Man occasioned so little psychological flutter and in many quarters awakened so warm and enthusiastic a welcome. They also serve to explain why it is so difficult to assign with confidence the precise contribution of Darwin's thought to current conditions in psychology. Many convergent forces have been at work and the independent effects of each are hardly to be discriminated. Nevertheless, it is clear that Darwinism exercises a very potent influence in psychology, not alone as regards general standpoint and method, but also as regards certain specific doctrines.

In the matter of general method we may certainly attribute to Darwinism thc larger part of the responsibility for the change which has brought into prominence functional and genetic psychology (including animal psychology), in distinction from the older and more conventional analytic psychology. Here again many influences have contributed to the final outcome, but it is fatuous to suppose that the genetic movement in psychology could have attained its present imposing dimensions had it not been for the inspiration of Darwin's achievements. The analytical methods will no doubt always retain a certain field of usefulness, and an indispensable one at that, but our larger and more significant generalizations, our more practically important forms of control over mental life are going to issue from the pursuit of methods in which growth, development and the influence of environment, both social and physical, will be the cardinal factors, methods which will in other words apply Darwinian principles with, let us hope, Darwin's tireless patience.

Darwin's more specific contributions to psychology may be grouped under three main headings: (1) his doctrine of the evolution of instinct and the part played by intelligence in the process; (2) the evolution of mind from the lowest animal to the highest man; and (3) the expressions of emotion. This is the chronological order in which these topics were given publicity by Darwin and we may properly adopt it in discussing the problems involved.

The solution of the first issue, i.e. the genesis of instinct and the part played by intelligence in such genesis, bears primarily perhaps on the field of animal psychology, but it certainly has a very definite interest for human psychology as well. At first blush it might seem that instinct is altogether a matter of muscular activities and neural mechanisms and that mentality has little or nothing to do with it. But a closer inspection of the actual manifestations of instinct serves to disabuse one's mind of that impression. Not only are human instincts honeycombed with psychic influences, but even animal instincts show themselves variable and adaptive to specific situations in ways which hardly permit any other interpretation than that of conscious adjustment. Take the imperious mating instinct as an instance. Among birds of many species there is every evidence that despite the impelling force of impulse, the female exercises a very definite choice in which to all appearances psychical impressions are potent. But the question still remains whether intelligence is a true cause in the production of instinctive acts, or whether it merely comes in occasionally to modify them. Herbert Spencer is cited with questionable justice as representing one extreme opinion in this matter. It is alleged that he holds that instinct is simply compound reflex action and that it is always the precursor of intelligence. This is clearly the view of many modern physiologists and naturalists, of whom Bethe and Loeb are illustrations. From this standpoint consciousness is not essential to the formation of instinct. Among English and American writers G. H. Lewes and Cope represent the other extreme, maintaining that all instincts are originally intelligent conscious acts, from which conscious control has largely or wholly disappeared. Some authorities like Romanes have held that consciousness is at all times operative in instinct and that it is precisely the presence of consciousness which distinguishes instincts from mere reflexes. This general view held with sundry modifications by numerous writers, among others Wundt, is known as the 'lapsed intelligence' theory.

Darwin himself seems to have been less interested in the question as to whether mind is always present in instinctive reactions than in the question of its relation to the origin of instinct. His view seems to have been that instincts are in part due to the inheritance of useful habits consciously acquired, and in part due to the effects of natural selection operating on chance variations in conduct. Of the two he regards natural selection as the more important, because many instincts cannot have been inherited habits (e.g. those of neuter insects), and because the selection of slight variations in action through many generations seems to him plausible by reason of the conclusive evidence of a similar process in the evolution of structures.

Against the natural selection argument, as it pertains to the supposed preservation of incremental variations of a useful sort, it has been urged that in not a few instincts this is an impossible assumption, because the whole value of the instinct depends on the appropriate execution of each step in a long series of acts, each one of which alone, and any group of which apart from the others, is useless. Natural selection could only furnish an adequate explanation provided the whole series of complex acts sprang into existence simultaneously. To suppose that this occurs is to assume the miraculous. Stated abstractedly this criticism appears forceful, but in view of our profound ignorance of the stages through which complex instincts have actually passed, it seems wise to be conservative in estimating the significance of the criticism.

It will be noted also that Darwin speaks quite explicitly of his belief that acquired habits are transmitted. The doubt which attaches to this doctrine in the minds of competent contemporary zoologists is well known. Darwin quotes as illustrating his point the alleged acquirement of fear of man by birds in certain of the oceanic islands remote from the mainland subsequent to the coming of men and the pursuit of hunting. Certain cases of alleged transmission of characteristics as a result of mental training among dogs appear also to have weighed heavily in his mind.

If such acquirements are transmitted by heredity, then it must be admitted that this factor, together with the natural selection of such instinctive variations as arise naturally and after the manner of structural variations, would no doubt largely account for the phenomena with which we are familiar. But as we have just pointed out, difficulties beset both parts of this program.

A compromise view which is put forward with the joint authority of Morgan, Osborn and Baldwin, under the title 'organic selection,' maintains that consciously acquired habits are probably not directly transmitted, but that consciousness plays an indispensable part in the drama by enabling successive generations of creatures to accommodate themselves to the vicissitudes of life while the slow changes are taking place which finally issue in the completed instinct. Not only is consciousness operative in this way, but in all the higher forms of animal life it is held that conscious imitative activities also play a part, and with man a dominant part, in setting the racial pattern. Natural selection serves to lop off the feeble and incompetent, both among individuals and groups, while all this process is going forward, but the successful issue is fundamentally dependent on conscious reactions during the critical formative stages.

In the midst of uncertainty and speculative ingenuity such as this, many minds will look with hope and a certain relief on the efforts of a group of zoologists and physiologists — illustrated by Jennings and Loeb — who have made persistent and in no small measure successful attempts to modify instinctive behavior by experimental methods, thus securing at once some rudimentary insight into the mechanics of the instincts, instead of waiting for nature to reveal her secrets at her pleasure. In the lower organisms where such experimental control is most feasible, already the dependence of certain forms of instinctive behavior on conditions of temperature, light and oxygenation has been demonstrated and it hardly seems unduly optimistic to hope that through such means we shall ere long be able to substitute for speculative theories on the modus operandi of instinctive behavior something more nearly resembling knowledge. At present we can only say that we know with reasonable certainty that many instinctive acts are accompanied by consciousness, that practically all of them are variable within limits, that some of them appear to be modified by conscious forces, that possibly consciousness has played a part in the formation of some of them as it seemingly plays a part in their actual workings, that natural selection would certainly account for many instincts and perhaps for all.

We come now to consider Darwin's view of mental evolution.

Darwin held that the mind of civilized man is a direct outgrowth of the animal mind. He maintained that from the lowest animal upward we find evidence of mental processes which increase in range and power, but do not change in kind, until we meet their most complete expressions in man. In man himself he finds again no evidence of aught but continuity of development from the lowest savage to the highest genius.

Darwin not only teaches the continuity of mental evolution from the lowest to the highest forms of animal life, he also urges the value of mental factors in the operation of both natural and sexual selection. Men and animals alike that were alert and intelligent in their adaptive acts would enjoy a larger chance of life and leave behind them a more numerous posterity. In those orders of animals where the female exercises selective control in the choice of a mate, he urges, as has already been indicated, that psychical factors enter in an important degree to determine the feminine preference.

His survey of mental characteristics on which these doctrines are based is somewhat naive. The psychic qualities which he cites as a foundation for his statements are as follows: sensations, pleasure, pain, passions, emotions (terror, suspicion, fear, anger, courage, timidity, love, jealousy, emulation, sense of humor, wonder, curiosity), imitation, attention, memory, imagination (whose presence in animals he regards as proved by behavior indicating dreams), and reason, which in animals, he says, is closely allied with instinct. These categories are all taken quite simply and with no special effort to indicate precisely what may be meant by them. He contents himself by citing illustrations of animal behavior, which seem to him to indicate the presence of these several mental attributes.

He undertakes to fortify his general position by a refutation of the several stock arguments commonly advanced to support belief in the radical distinction between animals and man. Of these we may pause to mention only a few

He meets the assertion that animals make no use of tools by citing the case of the chimpanzee who is said to use stones to open nuts, and by the case of the elephant who uses branches to protect himself from the assaults of flies. He might have cited many other similar cases, but it is to be observed that he makes no very satisfactory attempt to meet the further points that animals do not fashion utensils and that they do not use fire. For the present generation, however, this type of consideration has somewhat lost interest. He believes the opinion that animals do not form concepts and that they are incapable of making abstractions is not well founded. He cites as an instance of the appreciation by animals of something akin to an abstract idea, the attitude which a dog will assume in response to the exciting question, "Where is it?" The simple-mindedness of this conclusion must inevitably furnish amusement to the sophisticated animal psychologists of the present day. On the matter of language he occupies a position distinctly favorable to the possession of rudimentary language forms by animals. He cites the fact that many animals have calls expressive of emotion, and these calls he regards as essentially linguistic. He also mentions the use by parrots of significant words as a case demonstrating his contentions. Again, the sense of beauty has been held to be a purely human attribute. But this view Darwin feels is definitely controverted by the fondness which certain animals display, especially birds, for colors and plumage. The possession of conscience and the belief in God have frequently been urged as the sole possessions of humanity. To this assertion Darwin replies that the belief in God is not universal among human beings and hence not generically human, and the actions of many animals, notably dogs, indicate something closely akin to the feelings of conscience. To the contemporary psychologist all this sounds highly archaic and scientifically anachronistic and so no doubt it is- but in view of Darwin's extensive innocence of psychology, it represents, as he marshals his facts, an amazing range of original observation and a most intrepid mind.

In the last analysis, despite the statements of the preceding paragraph, Darwin regards the development of conscience, or the moral sense, as by far the most important practical distinction of man from the animals. He says, however, that any animal endowed with well-marked social instincts, such as the parental or filial affections, would develop man's conscience as soon as he developed man's intellectual capacity, or even approximated it. The social and gregarious habits of many animals obviously furnish an excellent point of departure for such a development. Moreover, sympathy, which plays an important part in all moral evolution, seems to be manifested by certain animals. There is therefore no evidence anywhere for radical differences between man and the animals.

It may be of interest to remark certain typical divergences from this general position in which, however, Darwin has found not a few loyal followers. Indeed, at the present time it is undoubtedly the case that most psychologists share Darwin's main convictions as to the continuity of mental evolution from animal to man, less perhaps as a result of careful scrutiny of the facts than as a consequence of a powerful drift from every direction toward the belief in a common origin for human and animal characteristics. We feel more comfortable nowadays in a world where simple and uniform rules obtain.

Probably the most persistent and most substantial point of dissent from Darwin is represented by writers who like Mivart hold that although men and animals have certain forms of conscious life in common, for instance, sentience and memory, man alone can frame true concepts, and man alone can use true signs, can create and use language. Only man has ideas. Whereas we find essential continuity from the lowest to the highest of bodily forms, in mental processes we meet a real break, separating the human and spiritual, from the merely sentient and brute.

This type of view has always commended itself to a certain stripe of religious belief because of its seeming provision for a somewhat super-naturalistic element in man, and its protest against regarding him, or at least his ancestry, as substantially on a level with the beasts of the field.

Moreover, it can summon to its support not a little apparently valid evidence wherein alleged instances of the animal use of language and signs are shown capable of another and more rudimentary interpretation. We are, of course, unable to intrude upon the inner workings of the animal consciousness, and it must be confessed that in so far as we judge by external conduct, few, if any, of the instances adduced to prove the formation by animals of concepts or of language really furnish unequivocal evidence of the thing to be proved. Meantime, it should be clearly recognized that this position, as advanced by Mivart at least, does not rest for its severance of man from the animals simply on the classical contention that he has a soul while they possess only minds. It is a distinction in the field of mind itself, which is here emphasized, an ascription to man, as his unique possession, of capacities which constitute the higher stages of cognitive activities.

Another divergent line is represented by the celebrated naturalist Wallace, who shares with Darwin a part of the credit for that revolution of opinion in the scientific world which generally is characterized with Darwin's name. Wallace is apparently willing to grant as a mere hypothesis that man's mind has developed pari passu with man's body, but he absolutely refuses to admit that natural selection could have brought this result to pass. He calls attention to three great familiar instances of alleged discontinuity in nature as suggesting that we should be scientifically hospitable to the idea of discontinuity. First, there is the breach between the organic and the inorganic, a breach which seems daily to shrink, but which has not yet been over-spanned. Then there is the equally marvelous break between the organic and the sentient, the conscious. And finally there is the break between mere sentience and rational intelligence — the distinction upon which Mivart dwelt so insistently.

Wallace cannot seriously call in question the possibility that natural selection should affect such mental qualities as quickness of eye and ear, accuracy of memory of former dangers and the like. It is the higher more definitely human qualities which apparently afford him foundation for his position. For example, what he calls the 'mathematical faculty' and the 'faculty for music' seem to him too remote from the life-subserving functions to have had any survival value, and unless they have such value, his position must be granted as having force against natural selection. On such grounds, in any case, he rests his contention that there is in man a spiritual essence not inherited from his animal forbears to whom he owes his bodily structure. By virtue of this essence human progress is possible and a spiritual life beyond the grave assured, for spirit cannot perish.

In reading Wallace one feels the presence of a vein of mysticism and the impelling influence of religious pre-possessions... influences which may properly be given a hearing, but which must not be treated as standing on the same logical level with ordinary empirical evidence. Whether natural selection can reasonably explain mental development in its higher ranges, is however, a perfectly fair question and one which deserves, and from ethical writers at least has often received, serious consideration.

It seems perfectly clear that certain familiar intellectual and emotional endowments would have had a very positive survival value both among animals and men. Those individuals who were mentally quick and inventive, who were courageous, cunning and pushing, would certainly be at an advantage over those who failed in these characteristics. Other things equal, the latter would live shorter lives and leave fewer progeny. When one takes into account the conditions of life under gregarious or social circumstances, one sees clearly how in a group the social virtues of sympathy, bravery, self-sacrifice, etc., may condition the dominance of the group over competing groups and consequently how a survival value may attach to these mental and moral characteristics. All this is familiar and trite and probably true. But what is to be said of Wallace's case as it concerns mathematical, philosophical and musical capacities, to the possessors of which men have customarily paid large respect? Wherein do such characteristics display a survival value, and if they have none such, how can natural selection account for their preservation and cultivation?

The reply, I believe, is quite in keeping with the reply as to the survival value of sympathy and pity and self-sacrificing bravery. In course of mental evolution, no doubt many characteristics are developed which are either harmful or useless. The congenitally insane illustrate the appearance of harmful forms. Other forms appear which may be useless or even harmful to the occasional individual, but to the group as a whole they are highly valuable and by virtue of this fact they secure perpetuity, either by social imitation, or by direct heredity. Now we have only to assume the appearance of a mental strain which has such social value, to expect with certainty that it will be encouraged in most of those who possess it markedly. Music and mathematics and philosophy do not represent such highly occasional mental sports as Mr. Wallace implies. A respectable amount of each of these capacities is latent in all normal individuals. Propitious surroundings are not always at hand and other more seductive interests often secure the field in advance, so that these capacities remain latent and undeveloped. But nothing is more certain than this: that if society did not at least consider itself benefited by the cultivation of these tastes, they would speedily disappear along with the taste for collecting scalps and wampum.

In other words, Mr. Wallace and others of his way of thinking take their natural selection too narrowly when they come to the higher ranges of mental life. They forget the social pressure which is there exercised, not to create but to develop certain capacities.

Still another view which not only accepts but magnifies discontinuity in natural phenomena is conceived not in the interests of any idealistic metaphysical or religious tenets, but rather in frank hostility to such. This is the view typified by Loeb, who believes that many of the lower organisms have no consciousness at all. This is a view which in more sweeping form Descartes long ago made famous, though on grounds quite different from those of Loeb. For Loeb, man's mind is a natural product of the evolution of animal mind, but animal mind itself begins not necessarily in the protozoa, but presumably at a relatively advanced point among the metazoa at a point where we find creatures able to profit by experience, able to learn.

Accepting the analogy of many chemical phenomena in which a critical stage is represented, before and after which the resulting phenomena are apparently entirely discontinuous (e.g., the formation of liquid from gas under given conditions of temperature and pressure) he urges that until precisely the correct molecular conditions are represented in the protoplasm of the nervous system, no consciousness will appear. But the moment these conditions are given, mind will also be present. It is not necessary to assume mind, or associative memory, as he prefers to call it, wherever we find a nervous system, much less wherever we find protoplasm in a living state. We have a right to allege the presence of mind only when the actions of an organism indicate its presence, and our only criterion for this presence is, as was above stated, the capacity to learn by experience, to improve the reactions made to stimuli.

The difficulty with this criterion is practical, not theoretical. If one could always say with assurance that animals can or cannot learn, the task would be easy. Unhappily such is not the case. Some animals learn to better a reaction after a few attempts; others require dozens of trials. Even the frog, whose intellectual capacities were once regarded as nil, has now been proved capable, under the advantages of higher education, of making some progress, but it is a progress which taxes both pupil and teacher, for it may require hundreds of experiences to improve even a very simple reaction. The criterion proposed, while theoretically admirable, leaves us as a matter of fact in much the position we occupied before: i.e. inability to confidently allege that any living creature is wholly lacking in mind. Even the lowly amoeba manifests certain peculiarities of action which may betoken consciousness of a low order.

An examination of these variants on the Darwinian view of continuity in mental development leads one to feel that the balance of probability distinctly favors the original formulation. Not only does modern psychology disclaim in man at least any such sharp lines between conceptual thought and the lower levels of sentient mental life, as Mivart and Wallace postulate, it has on the contrary expended no little effort in analyzing and defending the presence of just these conceptual processes in the sensory and perceptual activities of mind. Binet's essay on the psychology of reasoning is a typical example of this tendency, exhibiting as it does the implicit reasoning process involved in every definite perception. To perceive that this object before me is a desk, involves identifying this present visual experience with antecedent visual experiences in a way which closely resembles certain phases of the process in syllogistic inference. Nor has this tendency in psychology been in any way influenced by partisan Darwinian prepossessions, so far as I know. It has been the inevitable outcome of penetrating analysis. The use of conscious meanings does not suddenly burst forth full-blown in a mind which before had given no indication of such an achievement. The simplest mental acts which as human beings we can detect in ourselves have some increment, however small, of this consciousness of meaning, this embryonic form of conceptual thought. Nevertheless, it must not be forgotten that animals have certainly not been as yet proved to reason in human ways. On this score Mivart and his cohorts must be given their dues.

Nor is the dividing line which Loeb has proposed likely to result in any radical alterations in the general Darwinian position. For not only do we find it difficult to use the criterion Loeb offers - i.e. educability - but in point of fact we have considerable evidence at hand to show that even the lowest animal forms modify their behavior somewhat to meet changed conditions, and that these modifications are of a kind which in higher animals would be regarded as indicative of the presence of consciousness.

This brings us to the work on emotion. In his treatise on The Expression of the Emotions Darwin has brought together with characteristic patience and industry the most extended array of observations bearing on the subject, an array which has been of notable value to the defenders of the James-Lange theory of emotion. As finally put forth the work is a defense of three familiar theses concerning emotional expressions. The first holds that serviceable bodily reactions become habitual and become associated with the state of mind in connection with which they arose. When the mental state recurs, the bodily reactions recur also, although they may long since have lost any immediate and obvious utility. The clenching of the fist and the showing of the teeth in anger illustrate this conception. The second thesis, that of antithetic action, maintains that a state of mind opposed to one calling out a definite bodily attitude may evoke an opposite bodily attitude. As an illustration may be cited the fact that an angry cat naturally lashes its tail from side to side. On the other hand a cat which is pleased carries its tail erect and stiff. The third thesis, that of nervous overflow, holds that apart from the two previous principles of explanation, conditions of emotional excitement are prone to release more cortical energy than can be effectively disposed of in the usual ways, and the superfluity pours out in muscular contractions of the most various kinds.

So far as concerns the adequacy of these explanatory hypotheses, it may be said that in the light of our present knowledge the first affords a highly probable account of certain emotional reactions, while it is quite inadequate satisfactorily to explain, others. The second hypothesis has always been viewed askance, as something of a scientific tour de force, while the third, which Darwin himself treats rather as a catch-all to take care of cases found bothersome to handle by his first two hypotheses, is probably of much more fundamental import than he imagined. In any event later writers have been unable to improve materially upon Darwin's catalogue of the causative influences provocative of our emotional attitudes.

In conclusion we may venture a brief comment upon the methods now current in the study of evolving mind and more particularly upon the methods and points of view now dominant in animal psychology. A few words may also be added upon a group of problems suggested by Darwin's work.

The most marked and unmistakable change which we notice in method is the somewhat aggressive skepticism now everywhere entertained for the anecdotal foundation on which many of the early zoological doctrines about animals were based. Darwin himself quotes numerous tales to substantiate his positions and his disciples have far outdone the master. This condition of things has led not unnaturally to a reaction in favor of laboratory experiments and observations under conditions of control. To this procedure there is never lacking acrimonious protest on the part of those who hold that only under the conditions of nature can the intimate facts of animal life be seen and understood. No doubt there is a large measure of justice in this protest. But fortunately it is now possible in many of our laboratories and zoological stations to simulate with large success the conditions of life which are natural to many animal forms. The result has been a wealth of new material which promises quite to revolutionize many phases of animal lore. It seems not unreasonable to anticipate that the effect of such work will not only be felt in the direct increase of our reliable information gained through these channels, but also that the observation of animals in a state of nature will be rendered far more intelligent and precise by virtue of the suggestions which will be gained from work of this type. Certainly such work has already brought us new and more exacting standards of accuracy and taught us an invaluable caution and conservatism both in inference and in generalization.

Conspicuous among the many interesting psychological problems suggested by Darwin's work is that of the determination of mental types, species and genera, following rudely the analogy of species and genera in zoology. The practical difficulty in defining a species need occasion us no concern, because the idea of species has had great value, despite the perplexities attached to the satisfactory differentiations of particular classes. If the type of intelligence manifested by an animal be contingent upon the structure of its nervous system, as is apparently the case, it would seem to follow as a reasonable inference, that we might expect to find groups of animals evincing in their behavior psychic characteristics of a similar pattern, just as we find forms of nervous system highly similar to one another. It is of course conceivable that in different animals different nervous structures should function to produce similar psychic behavior. But even recognizing this possibility, it still ought to be feasible to group creatures together as belonging to various great psychical type-forms.

At present the common divisions follow other lines. Animals which belong to the same family, e.g. the dogs, are thought of as resembling one another in general mental pattern and as differing from other animals partly in their instincts, but partly also in their capacity to learn non-instinctive reactions. This practical view of the matter leaves us with as many main patterns as there are genera and with no explicit and tangible description of any one. The other line of demarcation consists in cross-sectioning such a division as the preceding by distinguishing between such psychical characters as sentience, memory and reason, ascribing all these attributes to the higher creatures and denying one or another to the lower creatures. Amoeba may be thought to have sentience, but not reason and only dubiously memory. The pigeon has sentience and memory, but probably not reason, whereas men and possibly some of the higher animals have all three capacities

Obviously neither of these modes of classification affords us any real insight into psychic types. If Darwin's fertile investigations are to bear fruit in this direction in psychology, we must be able to portray the entire range of mental processes belonging to the great divisions of animal life, to show where and how these dividing lines part company with those which now bind animal forms together on structural lines. For ordinary zoological purposes the dog and the elephant have little in common except their mammalian hallmark. But in their psychic types they may be very similar.

Such types may clearly be grouped around various central factors. Animals in which the so-called 'distance receptors' (auditory, visual, olfactory) are well-developed, may present a pattern with the psychic life all grouped about these processes. In other animals the 'contact- and proprio-ceptive' organs may be the centers of psychic life and in consequence give rise to quite another mental pattern. In one or in both, the psychic operations may be of the most rudimentary and immediate sort, or they may, on the other hand, involve processes comparable with the simpler forms of human inference. The patterns may vary again in dependence upon the relatively large or relatively small amount of purely instinctive and reflex activity. They may vary with the phylogenetic antiquity of the form, newer types being more plastic than older ones. Many other principles of grouping will readily suggest themselves.

At the present moment we have the beginnings, but only the beginnings, of the necessary data for the solution of this general problem. We have learned, for example, that the mere presence of a sense organ does not argue such a use of it as casual inspection would suggest, much less such as is suggested by the analogy of human sense perception. We have accordingly learned caution in assuming that the sensory activities of animals involve the sort of consciousness which we know in ourselves. Indeed our whole tendency nowadays is to recognize and frankly admit, that inasmuch as we must infer the psychic operations of animals wholly in terms of their behavior, we are under peculiar obligation to interpret their activities in the most conservative possible way. We know that the 'try-try-again, method' is the one commonly used by animals in solving laboratory problems. But we are for the most part profoundly ignorant as to just what occurs when progress is actually made, what sensory avenues are most important for giving information and how far the counterparts of human inference may at times be present. To secure these and dozens of other items of information needful for the execution of the program proposed will require long years of patient labor. Nevertheless, until this work is done, we shall remain powerless to describe the great stages of developing mind. The task is eminently worthwhile and is certain to be accomplished. Only when it is accomplished will it really be possible to entertain an intelligent judgment concerning the fundamental contentions of Darwinism concerning the evolution of mind.

Harry Houdini

Arguably the greatest magician and escapologist the world has ever seen, Harry Houdini also studied and investigated "paranormal" behavior throughout his career. His motivation for doing so was very much along the lines of that driving modern anomalistic psychology, namely an attempt to offer non paranormal explanations for so called paranormal beliefs and experiences.

This great article on the subject by Houdini was first published in 1925.

How I Unmask The Spirit Fakers

While I was playing an engagement in a mid-western city late last spring, a newspaper reporter called on me at the theater.

"*Houdini,*" he said, "*there's a spiritualistic medium who has been in town for more than 25 years. Would you care to come round with me and look him over?"*

Now, telling me that a supposed genuine medium is in the same town with me is like informing an enthusiastic fisherman that he's near a trout stream. For 35 years - during my whole career as a professional magician - I have been studying and investigating so-called, psychic phenomena - spiritualism, occultism, clairvoyance, mysticism, telepathy and similar manifestations of apparently supernatural origin.

My investigation has been literally continuous. I never have dropped it for so long as a day. The practice of my profession has taken me to virtually every country on earth, and my travels have enabled me to observe and study the psychics of many lands. And my interest in the subject is more keen, if anything, today than it was when it first engaged my attention. This probably is because my interest in psychic phenomena is personal rather than professional.

I have pursued my investigations because I have found them a fascinating kind of scientific research, not merely because seeking to explain the mysteries produced by others may seem to bear some relation to the work of one who is himself a professional mystifier. Also, the really tremendous popular interest in occult phenomena that has sprung up in recent years has stimulated me in pursuing my investigations. Every day that I appear on the stage, hundreds of people in the audience ask me question regarding spiritualism, telepathy, and kindred subjects. Every day my mail contains hundreds of questions of the same sort.

The public wants to know whether there are such things as "*spirits*,' whether it is possible for one man by mere exercise of his will to transfer his thoughts intelligibly to the brain of another man, and so on and so on. And as a servant of the public, which every public performer undoubtedly is, I consider it my duty never to let a chance slip of obtaining authentic data on the subjects regarding which the public is looking constantly to me for information. So it was with eagerness that I accepted the reporter's suggestion that I accompany him and another man, who proved to be the county prosecutor, out to the medium's home.

Now, despite any impression that may have been created by my activity in exposing fraudulent mediums, in regard to spiritualism I am not a skeptic. Although I have found no genuine physical phenomena medium, by which I mean one who does not produce his effects by purely natural means that any trained magician can duplicate, I have still an open mind. I am willing to be convinced - even to believe, if a medium can demonstrate to me that he actually possesses true psychic power. And when I went to the home of that veteran medium it was with every hope that he actually might prove capable of establishing communication with the spirits of the dead. One who had sustained his reputation for more than a quarter of a century in the same city, I reasoned, well might be assumed to be genuine. Besides, I am far too busy to waste my time "investigating" self styled mediums, who generally are believed to be frauds.

Once again, though, I was disappointed. This medium was just another trickster. His "*psychic power*" was due to his ability as a conjurer. His methods, in short, were merely a crude adaptation of those by which professional magicians mystify audiences from the stage. He was exceedingly clever, but I had unmasked him before his séance was completed, and as a result he was arrested as a fraud. Moreover, after my exposure of this man, the police of the city began a drive against fake spiritualists, which resulted a few weeks later in rounding up 20 of these swindlers who prey upon the credulous, the grief-stricken, and the troubled.

This man was what is called a "*trumpet medium.*" The term probably requires an explanation. A trumpet medium is one who evokes the "*spirits*" with the aid of trumpets - cones of metal or other material that resemble the fog horns carried by the old-time sailing vessels. The trumpets ordinarily are placed on table around which the medium and those attending the séance sit in a "circle," each person clasping hands with those on his right and left.

Now, the medium, being part of the circle, apparently cannot move without those who are holding his hands being aware of it. Yet, as soon as the light in the room is extinguished, queer things begin to happen. You hear "spirit voices," you feel the tapping of "*spirit hands*" on your head and body; odd, tapping sounds, which you are informed are the sound of "spirit feet," are heard seemingly in the air, or on the walls and ceiling. You hear sweeping sounds, too, which you are told are made by "spirit garments." Sometimes the trumpets, which are distinguishable in the darkness because of luminous rings that are placed upon them, are seen to rise from the table and apparently float about the room.

To one who visits a séance for the first time, these effects are most uncanny. You are quite ready to believe that they are actually caused by "spirits." Certainly, you tell yourself, the medium, with both hands securely held, is unable to get free to talk through the trumpets, raise them in the air, or tap them on the ceiling.

Well, as one who for 35 years has been freeing himself from every sort of bond, encumbrance, and restraint that human ingenuity can devise - handcuffs, ropes, chains, straight-jackets, locks, bolts, prison cells, trunks, safes, and packing cases among them - please permit me to testify that for a medium to free himself from a spiritual circle and to get hold of the trumpet is child's play!

And that's exactly how the wonders of the trumpet medium are performed. The medium gets free of the circle - or releases one hand or foot at least - and proceeds to manipulate the trumpets. Sometimes it is a confederate who permits him to escape. Sometimes, as I shall show presently, he does it through his own cleverness. The "spirit voices" that you hear are the medium's voice, disguised, issuing from a trumpet. In the darkness it is virtually impossible to trace to their source the sounds of a faint voice distorted by the megaphonic effect of a trumpet. Try the experiment yourself, and see.

The "*spirit rappings*" and sounds of "spirit wings" are made by the medium's fingers against the side of a trumpet. The taps which the sitters feel are delivered by the medium with a trumpet. To touch the ceiling with a trumpet or to reach a sitter at the far end of the table, the medium lengthens a trumpet by attaching it to another trumpet by means of the mouth pieces, which are made to fit one inside the other.

Some trumpet mediums also produce "*spirit voices*" in the daylight. The medium holds the large end of the trumpet near his mouth, and whispers into the instrument without moving his facial muscles, while at the same time carrying on a casual conversation with the sitter. You've seen ventriloquist on the stage disguise the fact that they are speaking by much the same method.

The particular medium of whom I write performed most of the usual tricks with the trumpets. He also caused a guitar, placed on the table before him along with the trumpets, to be play while he sat with his hands apparent covering those of the persons who sat at his right and his left. He establish communication with the "spirit" of the son of one of the sitters, the "*spirit*" of an Indian chief, who Spoke pidgin English in a deep bass voice, and the "spirit of a French opera singer, who led us in singing "*Nearer, My God, to Thee.*"

I said before, I attended this séance in the hope that the medium might produce something in the way of a genuine spirit manifestation. His methods, though, were so like those of fraud mediums whom I had seen and exposed that I was surprised at having thought him genuine in the beginning, and feared he would turn out to be a trickster. And so, when the opportunity presented itself, I slipped out of the circle in which I sat and smeared lamp-black on the trumpets. I waited until the medium had completed his trumpet work; then I rose, drew and electric flashlamp from my pocket, and directed its rays across the table.

It was a startling, though somewhat comical picture that the sudden light disclosed. For there in the circle sat the medium holding the guitar above his head, and his hand and face were as black as a coal heaver's from the lamp-black I had used!

By an ingenious trick he had freed his hand to manipulate the trumpets and the guitar. "*You could feel it if I raised my hand, couldn't you?*" he had asked one of the sitters beside him, and, as he spoke, he actually raised his hand and did not put it back, but substituted an Indian relic - a stone - of about the size and weight of his hand, covered by a handkerchief as had been his hand. The sitter, feeling the weight of the stone upon his hand, supposed, naturally enough, that the medium's hand had been replaced after its withdrawal. On this trick rested almost entirely that medium's claim to the possession of psychic powers.

Thirty-five years among these vultures has convinced me that they are the most contemptible and the meanest criminals that walk the earth. The confidence man, the burglar, the pickpocket, the highwayman, and others who live by robbing their fellows, must take chances. They meet their victims on even ground and triumph through their wits, their strength, or their courage.

The fake medium, though, works with everything in his favor. His victims will believe in him. They are grief stricken by the loss of a loved one, un-nerved and troubled by financial reserves, distracted by the disgrace brought upon them by their wayward children. In their search for consolation, in their troubles, for guidance in their difficulties, they grasp at straws. And the medium adroitly worms their secret out of them, plays upon their fears or their grief, impresses them by elaborate hocus-pocus trumpet work, slate writing, spirit rapping, table-lifting, spirit photographs the like - quickly has then in his toils and strips them bare of everything they own.

In the sheltering darkness, which makes it impossible for the sitters to observe anything he does, it is not necessary for the medium to be even a clever conjurer. Tricks that in the light would bring him nothing but a laugh of derision, in the darkness are startling and inexplicable.

I have caught a medium lifting a table - he claimed, of course, that the spirits did it - by squirming upward in his chair until the edge of the table was caught by a hook attached to his belt, while a confederate raised it a corresponding distance on the other side. Can you imagine a stage magician getting away with anything like that? Or can you imagine a stage magician impressing an audience by having his assistant tap certain persons on the shoulders and run his fingers through their hair? Under cover of darkness, though, and masked by the cloak of religion, such ridiculous trumpery becomes most impressive.

I remember in Chicago, quite a few years ago, a medium who had gained a big reputation by doing nothing more remarkable than the last thing I mentioned. This medium was a woman. She insisted upon being firmly held during her séances. Yet as soon as the room was made dark, the sitters felt taps on their shoulders and other parts of their bodies. Fingers were run through their hair. Their watches were snatched from their pockets and thrown to the floor.

I attended one of this woman's séances and I was completely mystified. She seemed to have no accomplices. I knew she had not left her seat during her manifestations, for I myself was holding her. However, my experience and my common sense both told me that her work must be accomplished by some natural means, so the second time I visited her spiritualistic chambers I went prepared.

As soon as the light was extinguished I poured a bottle of indelible ink over my hair. In a few moments, as I expected there came a light touch on my head. I moved my head so as to encourage the caresses, and the "*spirit*" spent quite a little time in pulling my hair and disarranging it. And then, when the light went up, the secret of these mystifying manifestations was plainly disclosed, for the hands of a little old woman who sat in a far corner of the room - by far the most innocent appearing person present - were black with ink!

One thing that has impressed me with regard to almost all mediums that I have seen and investigated is their startling lack of originality. The methods that mediums use to impress and mystify dupes today differ in few essential particulars from the methods that were used by the first mediums who sprang up like mushrooms after 1848 in the wake of the famous Fox sisters.

The Fox sisters, Margaret and Katie, were the founders of spiritualism as we know it today. They were two mischievous children of eight and six respectively, who lived on a farm at Hydesville, N.Y. To frighten their mother they began dropping apples and making other similar noises on the floor of their bedroom while they feigned sleep. Later they learned to produce the sound of rapping by clever manipulation of their fingers and toes, and in a short time the superstitious country folk imputed supernatural powers to them.

An older married sister saw commercial possibilities in the odd accomplishments of the children, and exploited them widely. That was the beginning of spiritualism, and, although Margaret Fox made a full confession in 1888, explaining in detail how she and her sister had fooled the public for years, spiritualism has continued to endure and the number of mediums has creased steadily.

Another point that I have noted with regard to mediums, a circumstance that should give any thinking person Pause before accepting as genuine the manifestation he witnesses, is that no "*spirit*" materialized by a medium ever offers anything that is above the mental level of the medium. All spirits, that is, talk in character with the medium.

Thus, I have heard an alleged spirit of George Washington speaking with an unmistakable cockney accent. I have heard the "*spirit of*

Shakespeare" make grammatical errors and use modern slang. It was something of that sort that caused me first to doubt the good faith of the average medium. When was about 16, I attended a series of séances given by a medium - a tailor - at Beloit, Wis. At the time I was a confirmed believer in spiritualism. This medium had impressed me greatly by the fact that he habitually put his sitters in touch with the spirits of great men - George Washington, Abraham Lincoln, Napoleon, Columbus - his séances were a constant panorama of history.

On the night that the "*spirit of Lincoln*" began to address us, my interest mounted high, for Lincoln was my hero of heroes. I had read and studied every Lincoln book that was available at the time. I knew every published detail of the Great Emancipator's life. And I was vaguely conscious that night of something about the utterances of the "*spirit*" that did not ring quite true. So at last I asked:

"*Mr Lincoln, what was the first thing you did after your mother was buried?*" "*I felt very bad,*" *replied the* "*spirit*" *glibly.* "*I went to my room, and I wouldn't speak to any one for days.*"

Now, that reply probably would have been correct in a majority of cases, but it was not correct with regard to Lincoln. For Lincoln's first act when his father had buried his dead mother was to rush off to engage a clergyman to read a burial service over her grave - an act of respect which his father had neglected! And this was certainly not an incident which Lincoln was likely to forget - in the spirit world or elsewhere.

Although this happening did not shake entirely my faith in spiritualism, there-after I watched closely the methods by which the tailor-medium accomplished his effects. One thing I noticed was the no matter how many "*spirits*" talked at his séances, only three voices would be heard, and these same three voices were heard at all séances, no matter what "spirits" appeared. When I inquired from the medium the reason for this, he looked at me intently for a moment, then laughed in an embarrassed way and said:

"Well, you've caught me; but you'd got to admit that I do more good than harm by consoling sorrowing people who long for a message from their loved ones!"

Caught him! I had no intention of catching him! On the contrary, it came as a painful shock to me that one whom I had trusted and believed in completely should so readily confess himself a fraud. When I had asked him about the voices and an odd hissing noise I frequently had heard in the trumpets which he used, I had been innocently seeking information about what I regarded as my religion. However, I was quick-witted enough to take advantage of his unexpected revelation. I permitted him to infer that I had been on to him all along.

"But, surely," I asked, "all mediums are not like you? There must be some genuine ones?" "None that I know of," he said with grin. "They're tricksters - every one of them!"

And it is with sincere regret that I must report that my 35 years of investigation of mediums in all parts of the world have given me no reason to doubt the statement the tailor-medium made to me then.

For years I have offered - with never a successful challenge - as much as $10,000 to any medium who can produce under conditions laid down by me any physical manifestation of his boasted psychic powers that I cannot duplicate by the methods I use as a professional magician.

For years I have been duplicating the most mystifying feats of the mediums from the stage - and then explaining to the puzzled audiences exactly how the tricks are accomplished. My success in this work has caused believers in spiritualism to declare that I am a psychic - a medium - without realizing it myself. Such a statement is of course absurd. Every feat that I ever have performed on the stage or off has been accomplished by purely natural means that are explainable by the laws of science and that would be understandable to anyone to whom I chose to divulge my secrets.

Once when a spiritualist was endeavoring to convince me that "*spirits*" aided me in performing the "escapes" that are part of my theatrical routine, I said to him:

"*My friend, for many years I have been forced to sleep with a pillow under my back. That's because a gang of longshoremen crushed one of my kidneys with a chain while tying me up on a stage at Buffalo, N.Y. Why weren't the spirits on hand to help me then?*"

He couldn't answer the question of course, but I am quite sure if he is still living, he is still a spiritualist. For I have found that the objections one offers spiritualists - even the most unfounded beliefs - usually have scant effect. Spiritualists will believe - those of them, that is, who are not frauds, for I have encountered only two kinds of spiritualists - tricksters and the deluded persons upon whom they prey.

And the latter are not to be shaken even by proofs that the "psychic manifestations" of mediums are accomplished by trickery. Mediums that I have caught red-handed - or black-handed, as the Cleveland medium I told above - invariably have found stalwart defenders among those whom they have been fooling. After I had exposed trumpet medium in New York City a few weeks ago, one of the medium's dupes attempted to attack me physically and only desisted on learning that police were in the room.

The spiritualist believers have a stock excuse for a medium who is detected in trickery.

"*Well, yes,*" *they admit,* "*you caught him that time - but that was because he had suddenly lost his power. It's only in such cases that he's forced to resort to trickery.*" For 35 years I have been encountering that kind of logic. It has been a severe test of my patience.

Even so noted a man as Sir Arthur Conan Doyle, author and scientist of world-wide reputation, creator of Sherlock Holmes, probably the most coldly, rigidly logical character in English fiction, many times has used much the same sort of specious reasoning when I have challenged the basis for his faith in spiritualism.

He is one who firmly insists that my stage tricks are performed with the aid of spirits; that I am a psychic. Once he went so far as to ask if I was "*the last word in religion and science in America.*"

"*Well, Sir Arthur,*" *I replied* "*not exactly that. But, if you were to build a packing-case large enough to contain me and all the American spiritualists and the scientists that uphold them, weight it with pig iron, tie us up in it and throw it into the sea, I'd be the only one that would come up. But it would be trickery that would release me,*" I added.

Frequently you will hear someone speak of a medium like this:

"*He must be genuine. Why, the spirits that talked in his place told me things that nobody but myself knew.*"

Bunk!

Early last summer Police Commissioner Enright, of New York, asked me to lecture at the New York Police Academy, to explain to the members of the police force just how to go about detecting fraudulent mediums. The best and most direct way that occurred to me of doing this was by staging a séance, performing myself the tricks that the mediums use.

After a little hocus pocus to add solemnity to the occasion - my séance by the way, was performed in broad day light - the "*spirit*" with which I alleged I had established communication asked:

"*Is Lieutenant Smith of the Eighteenth Precinct here?*"

Much mystified, the lieutenant acknowledged his presence.

"*I*," said the "*spirit*," talking through me, of course, "*am the spirit of John Brown, whom you saved from drowning at the foot of East Ninety-First Street in 1920. I want to thank you for that and congratulate you on your promotion. There'll be another promotion coming to you soon. Tell your boy Joe not to worry about his examinations; he's going to pass. And tell your wife not to worry about the baby. The little girl will get through the hot weather all right.*"

Lieutenant Smith had never spoken to me in his life, nor I to him, so naturally he was thunderstruck when the "*spirit*" singled him out from the big crowd of policemen present to tell him all this.

No doubt you, too, would be similarly astounded were I - or a medium - to tell you something similar under similar conditions. And yet there is nothing astounding about it. I was able to call that lieutenant by name because I had learned his name from one of his brother officers. I was able to tell him about the rescue because the same officer had told me about it.

My informant also told me the Lieutenant Smith had been promoted recently, that he was married, and the he had a boy of 12 and an infant daughter. Inasmuch as the schools were schedule to close for the summer in a couple of weeks, it was easy for me to guess that Joe was worried about passing his examinations. And since summer we coming on, I was quite safe in assuming that Mrs. Smith, like every other mother I've ever met, would be concerned about how her baby was going to stand the hot weather.

Simple, isn't it? Yet how mystifying when you're not in on the secret!

A favorite dodge of the mediums, that one! Almost invariably they work it on newcomers to their séances. Sometimes the surprising personal details related by the "*spirit*" are supplied by the spiritualist friend who has introduced the visitor, for spiritualists like to make coverts, and if they can do so by helping the medium in his trickery, they'll do it.

Give a clever medium a man's name, address, and occupation - information that can be obtained from the city directory - and with the aid of a few leading questions and a little deduction, the medium can convince that man that he knows the innermost secrets of his soul. I do this sort of thing from the stage regularly as part of my work of exposing the tricks of fraudulent mediums. One of my most useful pieces of equipment in this connection is a library of city directories of the leading cities of the United States. With their aid I am able to tell persons in the audience most astounding things.

Thus, while playing in New York recently, my assistant, whom I had stationed in the lobby for the purpose, related to me a brief exchange of conversation between two men, overheard while they were passing through the lobby of the theater.

"*Well, Mr. Blank*," one said to the other, "*how are things out in St. Louis?*"

"*Pretty good*," replied the other; "*we've sold a lot of cars this year.*"

With this much to guide me, it required only a moment to ascertain from the St. Louis city directory the full name and address of a Mr. Blank - the name I use is fictitious - who was in the auto mobile business in that city. Later from the stage I called Mr. Blank by name told him his business, made the obvious guess that it was business that had called him to New York, gave him the assurance of the "*spirits*" that his business trip would be successful, and otherwise astonished him and the audience by my supposedly spirit-given knowledge of his personal affairs.

At another performance in the same theater I absolutely flabbergasted a man in the audience by calling him by name, and informing him that he had come to the theater to escape from a quarrel he was having with his wife.

I knew this because I myself had observed the couple quarreling on the side walk before the performance began, had heard the wife call the man by name, and had seen him rush into the theater and buy a ticket.

On account of the prominence of the persons named, a demonstration of this sort of mediumistic trickery which I gave in a Boston theater not long ago cause quite a stir.

"*Is John Lewis Bates in the audience?*" I asked from the stage, naming a former governor of Massachusetts. Governor Bates acknowledged his presence.

"*The spirit of the late Governor Curtis Guild is here," I announced. "Probably you don't believe this, but I'd like to convince you. The spirit wants to know why you cut off the side whiskers you used to wear. You used to wear side whiskers, didn't you?*"

"*Many years ago*," replied the ex governor.

"*The spirit also wished to know if you recall having dined with him at the Algonquin club in Boston when he was governor about 20 years ago.*"

"*I recall it very well*," was the response "*He wants to know if you recall the subject discussed. It was Jesse Pomeroy, wasn't it?*" I asked.

"*Yes*," replied Mr. Bates, thoroughly astonished, while the audience gasped in amazement. "*But how did you know?*"

The explanation is almost unbelievably simple. I knew, of course, that former Governor Bates was in the audience. I also knew that he had formerly worn side whiskers, for I had seen him wearing them on another visit to Boston about 25 years ago. Also, former Governor Curtis Guild, journalist and soldier, was my personal friend. I had been his guest at to Algonquin Club in Boston. He had told me that it had been a customary procedure to present a petition for the pardon of Jesse Pomeroy, the famous boy murderer, to each successive governor of the state. Knowing all this, it was easy for me to piece together the tale I unfolded to him from the stage that night.

A few facts, and a little artful guessing - that is all the material a clever medium requires to mystify the average person.

26. A FACE FOR RADIO, UNIVERSAL EMOTION AND NAKED APES

"Fie, fie upon her! There's language in her eye, her cheek, her lip, Nay, her foot speaks; her wanton spirits look out At every joint and motive of her body."

(William Shakespeare - Troilus and Cressida, Act IV, Scene V)

I'm not sure who first coined the phrase "*Image is everything,*" however, I would hazard a guess that it was on the 26th September 1960 that the phrase first seared into public consciousness; as it was on this day that over 60 million Americans watched the first-ever televised debate between the presidential candidates running for the White House. At the time of the debate, Republican candidate Vice President Richard Nixon was recovering from a two week stay in hospital following a major knee operation. Looking pale and underweight he refused to wear any make-up to help enhance his complexion. In contrast, the Democratic candidate, Senator John F Kennedy looked a tanned picture of health after recent campaigning in California.

An overwhelming number of people who watched the debate on television stated that Senator Kennedy had won the debate outright; interestingly, however, the census of opinion among those who listened to the debate on the radio was that it was too close to call. It really is worth watching the debate to appreciate just how striking a difference there is in the image being conveyed by the candidates. You can see for yourself via the following link.

www.jfklibrary.org/Asset-Viewer/LYj_UVJ9gEyA5U9buPW8Hg.aspx

The Nixon-Kennedy debate is not only a classic case study in impression management but also a powerful example of just how important body language can be. Interest in nonverbal aspects of communication has a very long history indeed. In 1605, the English philosopher, politician and scientist, Francis Bacon had this to say about gestures of the body.

Aristotle hath very ingeniously and diligently handled the factures of the body, but not the gestures of the body, which are no less comprehensible by art, and of greater use and advantage. For the lineaments of the body do disclose the disposition and inclination of the mind in general; but the motions of the countenance and parts do not only so, but do further disclose the present humour and state of the mind and will.

For as your majesty saith most aptly and elegantly, "As the tongue speaketh to the ear so the gesture speaketh to the eye." And, therefore, a number of subtle persons, whose eyes do dwell upon the faces and fashions of men, do well know the advantage of this observation, as being most part of their ability; neither can it be denied, but that it is a great discovery of dissimulations, and a great direction in business.

In terms of a psychological appreciation of nonverbal behavior, look no further than Dr. Paul Ekman whose seminal research into universal versus culture-specific expression and gesture in the 1960's was nothing short of revolutionary. The prevailing consensus at the time - particularly within influential anthropological circles - was that facial expressions were culture specific. The opposing - but generally dismissed - universal argument was that there is an innate biological component to facial expressions - a view most famously espoused by Charles Darwin during his treatise on the expression of the emotions in the 1870's.

In 1968 Ekman set out to settle the debate whether facial behaviors associated with emotion are universal or culture specific. In a series of groundbreaking research publications co-authored with Wallace Friesen he found strong evidence in support of the hypothesis that the association between certain facial muscular expressions and discrete emotions is universal. Ekman's research based on film footage taken of people from an isolated area of New Guinea was particularly compelling; as Ekman himself notes "*These people have not been contaminated by the media or by contact with the outside world...They had never seen a photograph...There were, of course, no mirrors, so they had never seen their own faces...But I never saw an expression I hadn't seen before. There was nothing new. And whenever I could look [in the films] at what happened next [after the facial expression], my interpretation of the expression fits the social context."*

In a body of work spanning over 40 years, Paul Ekman has help redefine our understanding of the expression and physiology of emotion. The American Psychological Association named Ekman as one of the 100 most influential psychologists of the 20th century and he was selected by Time Magazine as one of the 100 most influential people of 2009. His role as a scientific consultant on the TV series *Lie to Me* and his collaboration with the Dalai Lama on emotional awareness is testament to Dr. Paul Ekman's enduring influence.

Dr. Desmond Morris: Pioneer in the Scientific Understanding of Body Language

Dr. Desmond Morris was born in 1928 in Wiltshire, England. An accomplished artist, film maker, world renowned TV presenter and author, he obtained a First Class Honours Degree in Zoology from Birmingham University in 1951 and was awarded a D.Phil. degree by Oxford University in 1954.

His first paper on animal behaviour was published in 1952, followed by the publication of a further 47 scientific papers over the next 15 years. In 1967 Dr. Desmond Morris published his first book on the subject of human behaviour. 'The Naked Ape', a zoologist's study of the human animal. The book is a sensation and goes on sell over 10 million copies worldwide.

A Personal Highlight

In March 2013 along with my good friend Craig Baxter, we got to interview Dr. Desmond Morris for our body language website. Below are a selection of questions and answers from that interview.

As a pioneer in the field of human body language, by definition, you wouldn't have had an established body of knowledge to draw upon when you first developed an interest in the topic. With this in mind, how did you initially go about formulating your ideas?

In the 1960s I commented that there were many dictionaries of words but none dealing with actions. As a student of animal behaviour I had previously been studying species where there were no words. Actions, movements, postures, signals, displays - these were the things that I was analyzing in fish, birds and mammals. When I turned to the human species I used the same method - direct observation of what people do, rather than what they say. I set out to make a complete 'ethogram' of human behaviour - that is to say a complete record of every action that a human being is seen to make. I am still working on that.

In your ground breaking book Manwatching, first published in 1977, you state that "as with all scientific research there is, of course the danger that new knowledge can lead to new forms of exploitation of the ignorant by the knowledgeable." 36 years on, would you say that this danger was realised. And if so, how?

Those with a deep understanding of human body language will

always be in a better position to interpret the feelings, motives and machinations of others. How they use this is up to them. Con men are good at this, so are magicians; also the best poker players and the best police interrogators.

Of all the places you have visited, which culture's body language and non-verbal communication did you find the most fascinating and why?

Italy. When Italians argue with one another their hands are as eloquent as those of orchestra conductors. And Japan, where the body language is so different, so precise, so disciplined. They find the expansive asymmetry of Western body language very clumsy.

You mention that in 1967 your bestselling book 'The Naked Ape' caused an outrage. What was the nature of this outrage? And do you think it would court as much controversy if The Naked Ape were being published for the first time today?

It caused an outrage because, at the time, it was generally believed that everything human beings do is the result of learning. I argued that a lot of human behaviour is the result of a set of genetic suggestions. Today this view is widely accepted, but not when THE NAKED APE first appeared. Also some people were insulted at being called animals. I saw it differently. For me, to be called an animal was a compliment.

What has been your proudest achievement in the field of human behaviour and why?

I do not allow myself the luxury of pride. I am my most severe critic. But I have to admit that seeing THE NAKED APE listed in "the top hundred bestsellers of all time" did give me a pang of pleasure.

If you would like to read our interview with Dr. Desmond Morris in full, see following link.

www.all-about-body-language.com/desmond-morris.html

Memoirs

The following extract is taken from the book Watching: Encounters with Humans and Other Animals. It provides a fascinating insight into how Dr Desmond Morris' human body language studies began. Many thanks to Dr. Morris for granting permission for it to be presented here.

After writing The Naked Ape I had come to the conclusion that there was something missing from the traditional studies of human behaviour. There were plenty of reports on abnormal behaviour, on tribal rites and rituals, on kinship structures and social institutions, on intelligence tests and learning processes, but there was very little indeed on the central subject of ordinary, everyday, human actions. The way we interact with one another in our homes and streets, in shops and restaurants, on beaches and buses, was rarely honoured with serious, observational analysis. Perhaps, for scientists, it was all too commonplace, too familiar. But by the same token it was at the very heart of what it was to be human, and I decided to make a stab at investigating it in a systematic way.

In my library there were dozens of dictionaries of words, but no dictionaries of human actions. To a zoologist this was a major omission. The first step one takes when starting to study a new species is to draw up an 'ethogram' — a complete, classified list of every type of action that the animal makes. In each case, the movement is carefully described, along with what causes it and what effect it has. In a moment of boldness bordering on arrogance, I decided to do this for the human species, treating it as though it were a new animal species, encountered for the very first time.

In attempting this I would employ a technique that was the precise opposite of the one employed by Sigmund Freud. When the great man had a patient lying on his famous couch in Vienna, he himself sat facing away, so that he could only hear his patient's voice, but could not set eyes him. I, by contrast, would only watch my subjects and would not listen to a word they said. I would confine myself entirely to non-verbal 'body language'. As a zoologist, I could not speak to an antelope or ask questions of a lion, so, treating humans in the same way, I would only observe and record.

One spring day [in 1969] I was sitting at a table in the main square of Malta's capital city, Valletta, sipping coffee and chatting to my publisher, Tom Maschler, who had flown out to discuss my next book. I explained what I was proposing to do, and he was slightly alarmed. An encyclopaedia of human actions seemed like a massive project, taking years and ending up almost unpublishable. But he encouraged me to make a start and see where it went.

We were watching an old man shrugging his shoulders. I pointed out to Tom that, unlike the English, the Maltese use a directional shrug. When an Englishman shrugs he directs himself forwards, at his companion, regardless of the subject being discussed. A Maltese, however, aims his hands in the general direction of the subject. If, for instance, he is complaining about something political, he will shrug his hands in the direction of the seat of government. If he is complaining about the lack of work in the docks, he will shrug towards the harbour, and so on. It was a tiny difference, but it made the body language of the Maltese subtly different from that of the English visitors to the island.

We continued to watch. The old man to whom the shrugger was addressing himself suddenly tossed his head backwards, closing his eyes and pursing his lips as he did so. If an Englishman did this, it would be a sign of irritation or scorn. But if this action is done by a Maltese it simply means 'No!' Again, a subtle difference. By spending hours observing the Maltese population, I had already come to understand a whole range of gestures and small communication actions that differ in some slight way from those of the country where I myself grew up. Strangely, though, I did not use these Maltese actions when I was talking to my Maltese friends. It would seem strange to perform a head toss instead of a head shake. But I understood the actions even though I did not personally employ them. This was rather like the condition a human toddler finds itself — understanding its parents words before it uses them itself.

As I kept up a running commentary on the body language around us, Tom remarked:

'You look at people like a birdwatcher looks at birds.'

'Yes' I replied, 'You could call me a manwatcher.'

'That's it,' said Tom, 'That's the title of your next book. We'll call it 'Manwatching''.

I was none too happy about this, still having in mind my big '*Encyclopaedia of Human Actions*'. But I made a mental note of it, all the same.

After Tom left I decided to set up a special office where I could start assembling my checklist of human body language. The Villa was big, but throughout the summer months it was always full of house-guests — friends taking holidays in the sun — and the atmosphere was wrong. I found a spacious office right on the Sliema sea-front, rented it and set to work. I took on an assistant, Trisha Pike, the lively, intelligent daughter of an Army officer who was stationed in Malta. We ordered a dozen huge boards, 8 feet tall by 3 feet wide, and stood them all around the walls. On these we planned to pin up hundreds of slips of paper. On each slip would be written one human action. We would then be able to juggle these slips around as we improved our classification system.

At first, it seemed a daunting task, but as the days passed, something was beginning to emerge. It turned out that human beings do not make as many different types of action as might be imagined. Because we could combine them in many ways and because we could vary their intensity, this gave a false impression that there were countless ways of using the human body. But if you simply took the basic elements involved, and classified those, the picture did not look so confusing.

To give three random examples: We only move our eyebrows in five ways — we raise, lower, knit, flash or cock them. We only cross our legs in four different ways — ankle-on-ankle, ankle-on-knee, knee-on-knee, or tight-twine. And we only fold our arms in four different ways — both-hands-showing; left-hand-showing + right-tucked in; right- hand- showing + left-tucked-in; both hands tucked in.

And so Trisha and I toiled on, pursuing our eccentric task of mapping the human ethogram. It took weeks, then months. The boards were now covered in hundreds of slips. At the same time, we were compiling files of photographs of all the actions. I was out recording actions on the streets, and every newspaper and magazine we could lay our hands on was being hacked to pieces. Slowly the repertoire of human actions was taking shape. It was amazing the way in which, once you had identified a particular action, it started coming up again and again, in the same sort of context. Nobody had ever named these actions before, so we had to do it ourselves. And the names had to be purely descriptive and could never imply a particular function or message.

After several more months it was clear that we were reaching saturation point. It would take a professional contortionist now to perform an action we had not identified and classified. And it looked as though there were about 3000 different actions that the human body performed in ordinary everyday life. I now started to write up my results, describing and discussing each action in detail.

At this point, Tom Maschler contacted me to find out how the new book is coming along. I announced proudly that I had reached the eyebrows. There was a pause. Then he asked: 'Are you going up or down?' When I reply 'Down' I sensed that he was not a happy publisher. After much debate it was decided that I should use my encyclopaedic records as the information base for some less ambitious books, and this was what I did.

The first book to emerge from this study was Intimate Behaviour. I then started work on the larger volume Manwatching, but it soon became clear that I needed to make field observations on a much wider range of cultures. In 1974 Ramona and I returned to England, where I took up a research post at Oxford, my old university. From there I began a new series of travels, with a team of 29 research workers and interpreters, exploring the body language of 25 different countries, right across Scandinavia, Europe, and the Mediterranean, an enterprise that proved to be highly rewarding, if at times slightly hazardous.

Gestures

Dr. Desmond Morris also very kindly provided us with some wonderful body language images. Here are two of them, along with an explanation of why he likes them so much.

These two images amuse me as examples of how easy it is to misinterpret gestures. The human one is Japanese, perhaps an early Samurai warrior, but what is he signalling? It looks superficially like the famous British insult signal, which is why is amuses me. But what is he really doing? Is he signalling two of something, or is he closely examining something that has stuck to his fingertips, or is he an archer who has hurt his bow fingers? Or are the two fingers, pressed tightly side by side, meant to represent a mating couple (as they do in some cultures). Or was there some other arcane meaning to this gesture among early Samurai? If they used it simply as an emphatic baton gesture it is very unusual example of a baton, having the third and fourth fingers held down by the thumb.

The monkey one is just a joke - an animal caught accidentally giving 'the finger'. Not to be taken seriously.

The two remarkable illustrations below are from one of the most precious books in Dr. Morris' library - John Bulwer's CHIROLOGIA, OR THE NATURAL LANGUAGE OF THE HAND published in 1644. Dr Morris considers these illustrations to be the most significant in the whole history of body language studies!

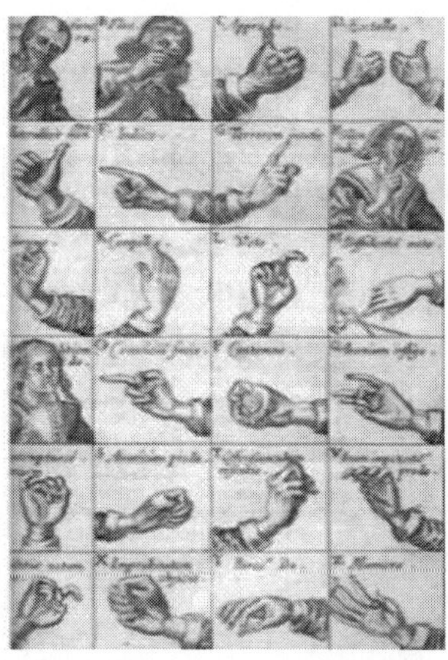

If you would like to see a much larger version of these illustrations, you can do so via the following link.

pinterest.com/pin/175218860227539337/

Learn More

A prolific writer and modern day polymath, Dr. Desmond Morris has produced a groundbreaking and accessible body of work spanning over 50 years. See following link to visit his official website.

www.desmond-morris.com

For free and comprehensive information on body language and non-verbal communication visit

www.all-about-body-language.com

27. I READ THE NEWS TODAY, OH BOY

This chapter showcases a selection of research both old and new which I came across and posted about online as a result of it having been reported upon in the mainstream media.

Here Comes The Rain Again Falling On My Head Like A Memory!

If a recently published study proves to be accurate then it follows that people living in Britain must have the best memory recall in the world.

In a simple recall test, researchers from The University of New South Wales found that participants were able to remember three times as many items on cold, windy, days as they were when conditions were bright and sunny. According to lead researcher Joseph Forgas:

"*We predicted and found that weather-induced negative mood improved memory accuracy...a worse mood helped to focus people's attention on their surroundings and led to a more thorough and careful thinking style, while happiness tended to reduce focus and increase both confidence and forgetfulness.*"

As somebody from Northern England who now lives in Southern Spain I would like to add my support to this research but I can't remember the reasons why!

Forgas, J.P., Goldenberg, L., Unkelbach, C. (2009). Can bad weather improve your memory? An unobtrusive field study of natural mood effects on real-life memory. Journal of Experimental Social Psychology, 45 (1), 254-257.

When you're Smiling

One of the reasons I love psychology is that it provides a fascinating insight into what it is to be human. Take something as simple as smiling for instance, we all do it (well most of us do and perhaps we've not been doing it as much lately) but have you ever thought about why you smile? I'm talking about a proper smile, not a false here comes the boss type smile.

Apparently there are two schools of thought concerning the psychology of smiling. These are:

1. Smiling is primarily an individual act. We smile as a result of an inner feeling of happiness.

2. Smiling is primarily a social act. We smile to let those around us know that we are happy.

So what do you think?

Ingenious Research

In attempting to answer the why we smile question, Robert Kraut and Robert Johnston from Cornell University decided to go bowling! Kraut and Johnston realized that happiness associated with good bowling, say bowling a strike or a spare provided the perfect opportunity to test the Individual vs Social smiling hypotheses.

The logic behind conducting research in this context is simple but brilliant. At the moment you bowl a strike you are essentially alone, you're not facing anybody, you're looking at the fallen pins, that happiness is all yours. Then shortly after you turn to face your fellow bowlers, family, team mates etc, it's time to share your happiness.

And the winner is?

Social smiling. 4% of bowlers smiled after hitting a strike or spare when facing away from fellow players compared to 42% of bowlers who smiled when they turned round to face other people having hit a strike or spare.

In discussing his research findings Robert Kraut stated:

"The smile is a facial response that is recognized around the globe and helps bind people together. We are indeed a "social animal," and the smile is a central way we communicate. I once did a study that blew up in my face because I asked a group of participants not to smile for three days – and they absolutely could not do it."

Kraut, R.E., Johnston, R.E. (1979). Social and emotional messages of smiling: An ethological approach. Journal of Personality and Social Psychology, 37 (9), 1539-1553.

The Psychology of Doodling

As a regular doodler myself, I was intrigued to read an article on the subject by science correspondent Ian Sample in the Guardian newspaper. It would be appear that far from being a futile exercise, doodling can in fact aid attention and recall. This vindication for all us '*doodlers*' out there relates to a research paper that was published in the journal of Applied Cognitive Psychology.

The paper entitled "*What does doodling do?*" by Dr Jackie Andrade, Professor in Psychology at the University of Plymouth (UK) found that participants who were randomly assigned to the doodling condition when monitoring a mock telephone message, performed better and recalled 29% more information on a surprise memory test, compared to participants in the control group.

In discussing the findings in the Guardian article, Dr Andrade is quoted as saying "*It's not so much that doodling is good for your concentration, but that daydreaming is bad. If you are thinking about where you are going to go on holiday, that is probably going to be more cognitively demanding than a doodle.*"

Andrade, J., (2009). What does doodling do? Applied Cognitive Psychology, 24 (1), 100-106.

Basking in Reflected Glory

Great story about research into the BIRG effect i.e., the tendency to "*bask in reflected glory*" (BIRG) by publicly announcing one's associations with successful others. In three field experiments conducted, the research team found that the BIRG effect occurred even though the person striving to bask in the glory of a successful source was not involved in the cause of the source's success.

Experiment 1 demonstrated the BIRG phenomenon by showing a greater tendency for university students to wear school identifying apparel after their school's football team had been victorious than non victorious and experiments 2 and 3 replicated the BIRG effect by showing that students used the pronoun "we" more when describing a victory than a non victory of their school's football team.

The BIRG effect was also observed by Professor Albert Harrison from the University of California when reviewing thousands of biographical entries in Who's Who. According to the biographical analysis many more people were born on Independence day, Christmas day and New Year's day than the days around these high profile dates. This statistical anomaly was apparently the result of some less than honest reporting by the great and good (including religious leaders!) who wanted to be associated with a nationally important day.

Cialdini, R.B., Borden, R.J., Thorne, A., Marcus, R.W., Freeman, S., Llloyd, R.S, (1976). Basking in reflected glory: Three (football) field studies. Journal of Personality and Social Psychology, 34 (3), 366-375.

The Say "Cheese" Guide To Avoiding Divorce

Whether you're looking for your soul mate or you think you've already found them, you might want to take a closer look at their photographs before you do the whole marriage thing, if the findings from a recently published study are anything to go by.

"Based on social–functional accounts of emotion, we conducted two studies examining whether the degree to which people smiled in photographs predicts the likelihood of divorce. Along with other theorists, we posited that smiling behavior in photographs is potentially indicative of underlying emotional dispositions that have direct and indirect life consequences. In the first study, we examined participants' positive expressive behavior in college yearbook photos and in Study 2 we examined a variety of participants' photos from childhood through early adulthood. In both studies, divorce was predicted by the degree to which subjects smiled in their photos."

Hertenstein, M.J., Hansel, C.A., Butts, A.M., Hile, S.N. (2009). Smile intensity in photographs predicts divorce later in life. Motivation and Emotion, 33 (2), 99-105.

B.F Skinner Discovers Shaping (As Luck Would Have it)

Glance at any list of the most eminent psychologists of the 20th Century and B.F Skinner will be towards the top of that list. B.F Skinner became the leading exponent of behaviorism within psychology. At the heart of this influential theory is the core belief that human behavior is best understood in terms of responses to environmental stimuli.

In formulating his theories, B.F Skinner conducted numerous behavior experiments with rats and pigeons and a central tenet of Skinner's theory was shaping. This is the notion that reinforcement can be employed to elicit complex behavior and behavior that would not normally be exhibited. It turns out, however, that Skinner's influential shaping procedure originally came about more by luck than judgment.

"Despite the seminal studies of response differentiation by the method of successive approximation detailed in chapter 8 of The Behavior of Organisms (1938), B. F. Skinner never actually shaped an operant response by hand until a memorable incident of startling serendipity on the top floor of a flour mill in Minneapolis in 1943. That occasion appears to have been a genuine eureka experience for

Skinner, causing him to appreciate as never before the significance of reinforcement mediated by biological connections with the animate social environment, as opposed to purely mechanical connections with the inanimate physical environment. This insight stimulated him to coin a new term (shaping)...Moreover, the insight seems to have emboldened Skinner to explore the greater implications of his behaviorism for human behavior writ large, an enterprise that characterized the bulk of his post-World War II scholarship."

Peterson, G.B, (2004). A day of great illumination: B.F Skinner's discovery of shaping. Journal of the Experimental Analysis of Behavior, 82 (3), 317-328.

Psychology on The Dance Floor

Back in 2009 I was reading about the various events that were going to be taking place as part of the Edinburgh International Science Festival and one in particular caught my eye. It read:

A dancer performs in total darkness. Points of light illuminate her movements. Is watching dance enough to make you feel like dancing? Take part in this live experiment investigating emotion perception and dance. No dance skills necessary, dancing shoes optional.

Given that I am officially one the worst dancers in the world I was intrigued to find out more. It turns out that this event was based on a research project by Professor Richard Wiseman and Dr Peter Lovat from the University of Hertfordshire, who building on the findings of a previous study were working alongside dancer Caroline Duker to investigate how dancers portray emotion. As part of the research design, participants watched a dancer perform the same routine either in full light, or in the dark with small points of light attached to the dancer's body. Participants then had to attempt to work out the emotion the dancer was portraying.

In discussing their initial findings Professor Wiseman noted.

"*In one part of the experiment, participants saw a dancer portray one of four emotions (neutral, joy, sadness, and anger) whilst performing in full light. The results showed that people were 80% correct. The second part of the experiment involved watching videos of the same dance sequences, but this time everyone just saw six light points that were attached to the dancers shoulders, wrists and ankles.*

The previous work had shown that people were about 63% accurate when shown 13 points of light. Remarkably, participants in our study were 62% accurate with just six points of light. This suggests that people can recognise emotional movement from just the smallest amount of information. We found no difference between men and woman, or different ages. "

Dynamic Emotion

Existing studies into the perception of emotion almost exclusively employed a static methodology i.e. still photographs of facial expressions. These fascinating results suggest that dynamic displays of emotion expressed non facially may be just as important and as such warrant further investigation.

Where the Hell is Matt? 2012

See following link to watch a video celebrating the universal joy of dance which has been viewed over 10,000,000 times.

www.youtube.com/watch?v=Pwe-pA6TaZk

Atkinson, A.P., Tunstall, M.L., Dittrich, W.H. (2007). Evidence for distinct contributions of form and motion information to the recognition of emotions from body gestures. Cognition, 104 (1), 59-72.

28. ALLOW ME TO INTRODUCE

I mention in the introduction that I have been sharing my passion for psychology online for over six years now. Thankfully, there are so many interesting people out there doing so many interesting things in the name of psychology that I never struggle to find something to post about. There are, however, certain individuals who deserve a special mention.

These are people who continually move the discipline of psychology forward by presenting informative, engaging and highly accessible material. These are people whose work I have featured regularly on both my psychology website and related social media channels and these are people who I continue to learn a great deal from. Whatever your connection with psychology - student, educator, professional or general interest; these are people who will make that connection considerably stronger.

Paul Bloom

Yale University psychology Professor Paul Bloom is a world renowned expert in how children and adults understand the physical and social world, particularly in relation to morality, religion, fiction, and art.

An award-winning researcher and teacher, Professor Bloom's work has been published in numerous scientific journals such as Nature and Science and he is the author of several books, including How Children Learn the Meanings of Words, Descartes' Baby, and How Pleasure Works.

Professor Bloom's introduction to psychology course is available to the public free of charge via the Internet. The official course description is as follows:

What do your dreams mean? Do men and women differ in the nature and intensity of their sexual desires? Can apes learn sign language? Why can't we tickle ourselves? This course tries to answer these questions and many others, providing a comprehensive overview of the scientific study of thought and behavior. It explores topics such as perception, communication, learning, memory, decision-making, religion, persuasion, love, lust, hunger, art, fiction, and dreams. We will look at how these aspects of the mind develop in children, how they differ across people, how they are wired-up in the brain, and how they break down due to illness and injury.

Make sure you take advantage of this outstanding opportunity to learn about psychology for free via the following link.

oyc.yale.edu/psychology/psyc-110

See following link to learn more about Professor Paul Bloom and to connect with him online.

pantheon.yale.edu/~pb85/Paul_Bloom.html

Michael Britt

Dr. Michael Britt graduated from The State University of New York at Albany with a Ph.D. in psychology and taught Psychology at Marist College (Poughkeepsie, New York USA) for 10 years. Dr. Britt is the host of the premier academic psychology podcast, The Psych Files. Always in the top 10 of the iTunes Higher Education category each episode of The Psych Files is downloaded more than 20,000 times, resulting in over 6 million downloads worldwide.

Dr. Britt is a pioneer of how technology can be utilized in the teaching and learning process, as seen in the innovative use of audio and video employed in the making of The Psych Files. The Psych Files is aimed at anyone curious about human behavior, though students taking a course in psychology, those majoring in psychology and instructors of psychology will find the podcast particularly useful.

See following link to learn more about Dr. Britt and to connect with him online.

www.thepsychfiles.com

Christopher French

Christopher French is a professor of psychology at Goldsmiths, University of London. His primary research area is the psychology of paranormal beliefs, particularly in relation to offering non-paranormal explanations for claims of paranormal experience through examining errors in human information-processing e.g. memory, perception, and judgment and the psychology of deception/self-deception.

In 2001, Professor French established the Anomalistic Psychology Research Unit in order to highlight the important research being conducted within this field. He appears regularly across the media to provide a skeptical perspective on various paranormal claims and writes a regular column in The Skeptic Magazine (UK). Professor French is also a columnist for the Guardian's online science pages.

See following link to learn more about the work of Professor French and to connect with him online.

www.gold.ac.uk/apru/

Claudia Hammond

Claudia Hammond is an award-winning broadcaster, writer and psychology lecturer. She presents the critically acclaimed *All in the Mind* and *Mind Changers* series on BBC Radio 4.

In *All in the Mind*, Claudia Hammond explores the potential of the human mind by showcasing the latest research and bringing together experts and commentators from the worlds of psychiatry, psychology and mental health; and in *Mind Changers* she examines the work of psychologists who have changed our understanding of the human mind. Both these series are wonderfully insightful and if you are a psychology student you will find them an invaluable source of information. See following links.

www.bbc.co.uk/programmes/b006qxx9 (All in The Mind)

www.bbc.co.uk/programmes/b008cy1j (Mind Changers)

A published author, her book *Emotional Rollercoaster* investigates the science behind fear, sadness, anger, happiness, disgust, hate, jealousy, love, sympathy and guilt. And her latest book *Time Warped* unlocks the mysteries of time perception. Claudia Hammond regularly appears on TV to discuss research in psychology, and is on the part-time faculty at Boston University's London base where she lectures in health and social psychology.

See following link to learn more about Claudia Hammond and to connect with her online.

www.claudiahammond.com

Christian Jarrett

Dr Christian Jarrett has a PhD in cognitive neuroscience and is a chartered psychologist and associate fellow of the British Psychological Society (BPS).

Dr. Jarrett has edited and written the BPS Research Digest since its inception in 2003 and created the associated BPS Research Digest blog in 2005. In producing this award-winning blog Dr. Jarrett reviews hundreds of peer-reviewed journals in order to report on the latest findings within psychological science.

I highly recommend taking a look at the BPS Research Digest blog, the primary aim of which is to evaluate important studies which are "*relevant to real life, timely, novel or thought-provoking.*" See following link.

www.bps-research-digest.blogspot.com

Dr. Jarrett is also a staff writer for The Psychologist magazine, a blogger for Psychology Today and a columnist for 99U, the New York-based creativity think tank. His book *The Rough Guide To Psychology* was a hit with reviewers and short-listed for two prestigious awards. His latest book, *Great Myths of the Brain* is due for publication in 2014.

See following link to learn more about Dr Christian Jarrett and to connect with him online.

www.psychologywriter.org.uk

Steven Pinker

Harvard Professor Steven Pinker is an experimental psychologist who is widely considered the leading authority on language, mind, and human nature. Professor Pinker has been named Humanist of the Year, appeared in Time magazine's "The 100 Most Influential People in the World Today," and most recently following over 10,000 votes cast in over 100 countries, was named in the top three winners of Prospect's world thinkers 2013 poll.

A prolific researcher, media commentator and author, Professor Pinker's books include *The Language Instinct, How the Mind Works, Words and Rules, The Blank Slate, The Stuff of Thought*, and his latest publication *The Better Angels of Our Nature: Why Violence Has Declined.*

See following link to learn more about Professor Steven Pinker and to connect with him online.

stevenpinker.com

Richard Wiseman

Professor Richard Wiseman started his working life as an award-winning professional magician, and was one of the youngest members of The Magic Circle. He obtained a first class honours degree in Psychology from University College London and a doctorate in psychology from the University of Edinburgh.

Professor Richard Wiseman holds Britain's only Professorship in the Public Understanding of Psychology at the University of Hertfordshire, where he has established an international reputation for his research into an eclectic range of topics including luck, self-help, illusion, persuasion and the paranormal. He has published numerous papers in leading academic journals, including articles in one of the world's most respected science publications, Nature.

A best-selling author, Professor Wiseman has written several books, including *59 Seconds, Paranormality, Rip It Up/The As If Principle, The Luck Factor, Quirkology, and Did You Spot The Gorilla.* His psychology-based YouTube videos have received over 120 million views, he has over 118,000 twitter followers and over 2 million people have taken part in his mass participation experiments. A much sought after media figure, Professor Wiseman has acted as a creative consultant to Derren Brown, The MythBusters and CBS's The Mentalist.

See following link to learn more about Professor Wiseman and to connect with him online.

richardwiseman.wordpress.com

Philip Zimbardo

Professor Emeritus of Psychology at Stanford University, Dr. Philip Zimbardo is a world-renowned educator, researcher, speaker and author. With over 50 books and more than 400 published articles to his name, Dr. Zimbardo has been informing our understanding of human behavior for over forty years. His landmark Stanford Prison Experiment in 1971 showed how situations and systems can make good people do bad things by creating the conditions in which those in positions of power dehumanize those in less powerful positions. These seminal findings continue to resonate today in what they tell us about contemporary events such as the Abu Ghraib prisoner abuses in Iraq; the resulting trial of which saw Dr. Zimbardo serve as an expert witness.

Dr. Zimbardo is a passionate standard bearer for the discipline of psychology. His ground-breaking public television series, Discovering Psychology has been seen by millions of people worldwide and received the Carl Sagan Award for Public Understanding of Science. He continues to pursue many important areas of research, for example he is currently involved in developing the theory of Social Intensity Syndrome, a new phenomenon related to long-term military socialization.

See following link to learn more about Professor Philip Zimbardo and to connect with him online.

www.zimbardo.com

29. CONNECT AND LEARN

"*The Web does not just connect machines, it connects people.*"

(Tim Berners-Lee)

Join me and thousands of fellow psychology enthusiasts online.

Psychology on Facebook

www.facebook.com/psychologyonline

Psychology on Twitter

twitter.com/psych101

Psychology on Google+

goo.gl/hU8JL

Psychology on Linkedin

www.linkedin.com/groups/Psychology-Students-Network-4016322/about

Psychology on YouTube

www.youtube.com/user/LearnAboutPsychology

Psychology on Pinterest

pinterest.com/psychology

The "ALL ABOUT" Website Portfolio

Explore the four websites built around my teaching and research interests.

www.all-about-psychology.com

www.all-about-forensic-psychology.com

www.all-about-forensic-science.com

www.all-about-body-language.com

Psychology Student Guide

Drawing on my experience as a student and then a lecturer in psychology, the Psychology Student Guide is designed for anyone who would like to learn more about what psychology actually is; anyone who is thinking about studying the subject or anyone who is currently a psychology student. See following link for full details.

www.amazon.com/dp/B009ZC2UOS

And Finally

After all this incredibly interesting psychology I'd like to finish with a boring quote!

"The most important and greatest puzzle we face as humans is ourselves."

(Edwin Boring)

3915350R00131

Printed in Great Britain
by Amazon.co.uk, Ltd.,
Marston Gate.